THE THREAT OF CHINA'S UNSAFE CONSUMABLES

HEARING

BEFORE THE

SUBCOMMITTEE ON EUROPE, EURASIA, AND EMERGING THREATS

OF THE

COMMITTEE ON FOREIGN AFFAIRS HOUSE OF REPRESENTATIVES

ONE HUNDRED THIRTEENTH CONGRESS

FIRST SESSION

MAY 8, 2013

Serial No. 113–25

Printed for the use of the Committee on Foreign Affairs

Available via the World Wide Web: http://www.foreignaffairs.house.gov/ or http://www.gpo.gov/fdsys/

U.S. GOVERNMENT PRINTING OFFICE

80–800PDF   WASHINGTON : 2013

For sale by the Superintendent of Documents, U.S. Government Printing Office
Internet: bookstore.gpo.gov   Phone: toll free (866) 512–1800; DC area (202) 512–1800
Fax: (202) 512–2104   Mail: Stop IDCC, Washington, DC 20402–0001

COMMITTEE ON FOREIGN AFFAIRS

EDWARD R. ROYCE, California, *Chairman*

CHRISTOPHER H. SMITH, New Jersey
ILEANA ROS-LEHTINEN, Florida
DANA ROHRABACHER, California
STEVE CHABOT, Ohio
JOE WILSON, South Carolina
MICHAEL T. McCAUL, Texas
TED POE, Texas
MATT SALMON, Arizona
TOM MARINO, Pennsylvania
JEFF DUNCAN, South Carolina
ADAM KINZINGER, Illinois
MO BROOKS, Alabama
TOM COTTON, Arkansas
PAUL COOK, California
GEORGE HOLDING, North Carolina
RANDY K. WEBER SR., Texas
SCOTT PERRY, Pennsylvania
STEVE STOCKMAN, Texas
RON DeSANTIS, Florida
TREY RADEL, Florida
DOUG COLLINS, Georgia
MARK MEADOWS, North Carolina
TED S. YOHO, Florida
LUKE MESSER, Indiana

ELIOT L. ENGEL, New York
ENI F.H. FALEOMAVAEGA, American Samoa
BRAD SHERMAN, California
GREGORY W. MEEKS, New York
ALBIO SIRES, New Jersey
GERALD E. CONNOLLY, Virginia
THEODORE E. DEUTCH, Florida
BRIAN HIGGINS, New York
KAREN BASS, California
WILLIAM KEATING, Massachusetts
DAVID CICILLINE, Rhode Island
ALAN GRAYSON, Florida
JUAN VARGAS, California
BRADLEY S. SCHNEIDER, Illinois
JOSEPH P. KENNEDY III, Massachusetts
AMI BERA, California
ALAN S. LOWENTHAL, California
GRACE MENG, New York
LOIS FRANKEL, Florida
TULSI GABBARD, Hawaii
JOAQUIN CASTRO, Texas

AMY PORTER, *Chief of Staff*   THOMAS SHEEHY, *Staff Director*

JASON STEINBAUM, *Democratic Staff Director*

———

SUBCOMMITTEE ON EUROPE, EURASIA, AND EMERGING THREATS

DANA ROHRABACHER, California, *Chairman*

TED POE, Texas
TOM MARINO, Pennsylvania
JEFF DUNCAN, South Carolina
PAUL COOK, California
GEORGE HOLDING, North Carolina
STEVE STOCKMAN, Texas

WILLIAM KEATING, Massachusetts
GREGORY W. MEEKS, New York
ALBIO SIRES, New Jersey
BRIAN HIGGINS, New York
ALAN S. LOWENTHAL, California

(II)

CONTENTS

THE THREAT OF CHINA'S UNSAFE CONSUMABLES

WEDNESDAY, MAY 8, 2013

House of Representatives,
Subcommittee on Europe, Eurasia, and Emerging Threats,
Committee on Foreign Affairs,
Washington, DC.

The subcommittee met, pursuant to notice, at 2 o'clock p.m., in room 2172 Rayburn House Office Building, Hon. Dana Rohrabacher (chairman of the subcommittee) presiding.

Mr. ROHRABACHER. I call to order this hearing of the Foreign Affairs Subcommittee on Europe, Eurasia, and Emerging Threats. Today's topic is ''The Threat of China's Unsafe Consummables,'' an emerging threat.

After the ranking members and I each take our 5 minutes to make opening remarks, each member present will have 1 minute to make some opening remarks as well, alternating between majority and minority members and without objection all members will have 5 days to submit statements, questions, extraneous material for the record. Hearing no objections, so ordered.

Who could forget that agricultural interests were the driving force behind various trading and trade-expanding understandings that our country has had with the communist Chinese regime in Beijing. Who would have thought that the People's Republic of China would become a significant food exporter, especially of fruits, vegetables, seafood, and dairy products? The farming community, the agricultural industry puts so much effort because they just saw this as a market for their goods, never did they consider that these would be competitors and competitors that did not have to meet the same standards that they have.

Chinese industry has also become a major producer of drugs and chemicals used in both medicine and food processing and yes, and in manufacturing as well. Thus, the health and safety not only of the United States and Europe, but that of people around the world has become dependent on the quality of goods imported from China. Yet, the task of inspecting and testing Chinese goods is beyond the ability of governments. Considering the magnitude of that challenge, it is beyond their ability to do a good job or at least that is what I am suggesting. We will hear from our witnesses what they think about that.

Astonishingly, the U.S. Food and Drug Administration inspects less than 2 percent of the food imports from China. This is a major security concern. Why? Because the record of Chinese quality in

(1)

their food production is extremely poor. Indeed, CNN reported Monday that poultry workers moving to and from wet markets and farms may be responsible for the spread of the deadly H7N9 virus in China, read that, the bird flu virus. We import poultry now to feed animals, but the FDA may soon approve the importation of China poultry for human consumption. Now does this move make sense at all?

Ronald Reagan once said of the Soviet Union, ''trust, but verify.'' In regards to Communist China, however, we cannot trust, nor can we verify. China producers are motivated to cut corners, dilute content, counterfeit products to maximize profits, and keep prices so low as to dominate export markets. Chinese supervision and regulation is weak and corrupt. We have the irony of a communist system that has spawned the most predatory capitalism of all. The result is food that makes you sick and drugs that will not make you well and could well kill you.

Even the state-owned media knows the problem. Last October, China Daily cited a marketing survey which found and I quote, ''Food safety is a top concern for Chinese shoppers, especially regarding such produce as vegetables, meat, seafood, grain, cooking oils, and dairy foods.'' If this is true within China, then it should also be true for foreign markets. And a series of scandals involving toxic chemicals and other fillers in food products around the world confirm this. Yet, Chinese agricultural exports continue to increase, driven by their low prices.

The same is true in the pharmaceutical industry. There has been movement, again unexpected, of much of that industry from the United States to China. Just like in the agricultural area we saw a whole industry shift over to China that was never predicted by agriculture, while it also hasn't been predicted by the pharmaceutical industry. Beijing has been allowed, for example, to join the World Trade Organization which helped this shift. This shift was motivated by a desire to cut costs by using cheap Chinese labor and by avoiding expensive regulation. This opened the door not only to lower quality output, but made it easier for counterfeiters to infiltrate the supply side and supply chains of our pharmaceutical products. Drugs with weak dosages or no active ingredients at all endanger public health and discredit treatment programs. Fake drugs undermine U.S. efforts to treat illnesses in developing countries. For example, the State Department has requested $650 million in 2014 to fight malaria in developing countries. Yet, half that anti-malarial drugs that are on the market in South Asia and Africa have been found to be counterfeit. And most of these fake drugs come from where? China.

Fakes also threatened the campaign against diabetes and other significant and debilitating diseases.

Besides the global health, safety, and security threats created by unscrupulous Chinese business practices and the corrupt lack of supervision by Chinese authorities, there is a competitive issue as well. American farmers are the most productive in the world and are held to rigorous standards. The same is true of the American pharmaceutical industry which creates the world's most advanced medicines. Yet, if U.S. exports are defeated in the market place on the basis of lower prices stemming from illicit cost cutting, then the American producer as well as our entire economy will suffer.

Counterfeit products are often sold under the brand new of the legitimate product such as Pfizer or Lipitor, or several others. Indeed, there has been and there is hardly an American company that has not been victimized by this Chinese larceny. And when the product does not work, the brand is held responsible. But yet it is not the people of that company that has been making the product. It is a knockoff by some Chinese company that has been permitted to do so by the Chinese authorities that should be enforcing the rule of law.

Now if you end up having a Chinese company under the name of another company, an American company or whatever, what we have done is we have slandered the name of an American company and we have slandered the ability of the people of the United States and our system as well because we have basically been at that point saying to the world this is what our products are like, but it is not our product. This is something we have got to stop if we are going to maintain the integrity and the trust that the people around the world have in American products. Not to mention we have got to stop it because there are people who are being injured and killed because they are using these phony products that are being manufactured by someone else other than who is on the label.

Are there measures we can take to persuade China not to do certain things or things that China can be persuaded to do to safeguard consumers from dangerous exports? Or what steps can we take or should we just ban all such goods from China from the marketplace because they are inherently unsafe. Well, that is a question we will have to talk about today. The production and distribution of such critical goods as food and medicine upon which life itself depends cannot be trusted unless there is integrity throughout the manufacturing and supply chains. We have gathered this panel of experts to help us decide what the policy options are.

[The prepared statement of Mr. Rohrabacher follows:]

OPENING STATEMENT

"The Threat of China's Unsafe Consumables"

Chairman Dana Rohrabacher
Subcommittee on Europe, Eurasia, and Emerging Threats
House Committee on Foreign Affairs

May 8, 2013

Who can forget that agricultural interests were the driving force behind the various trade expanding understandings that our country has had with the Communist Chinese regime in Beijing. Who would have thought that the People's Republic of China would become a significant food exporter, especially of fruits, vegetables, seafood and dairy products?

Chinese industry has also become a major producer of drugs and chemicals used in both medicine and food processing. Thus the health and safety not only of the United States and Europe, but that of people around the world has become dependent on the quality of goods imported from China. Yet, the task of inspecting and testing Chinese goods is beyond the ability of governments given the magnitude of the challenge. Astonishingly, the U.S. Food and Drug Administration inspects less than 2% of food imports. This is a major security concern because the record of Chinese quality is extremely poor.

Indeed, CNN reported Monday that "Poultry workers moving to and from wet markets and farms may be responsible for the spread of the deadly H7N9 virus in China," That's the "bird flu" virus. We import poultry now to feed animals, but the FDA may soon approve the importation of Chinese poultry for human consumption. Does this make sense?

Ronald Reagan once said of the Soviet Union, "trust, but verify." In regards to Communist China, however, we cannot trust nor can we verify.

Chinese producers are motivated to cut corners, dilute content and counterfeit products to maximize profits and keep prices low so as to dominate export markets. Chinese supervision and regulation is weak and corrupt. We have the irony of a Communist system that has spawned the most predatory capitalists. The result is food that makes you sick and drugs that will not make you well---and could kill you.

Even the state-owned media knows the problem. Last October, *China Daily* cited a marketing survey which found, "Food safety is a top concern for Chinese shoppers, especially regarding such produce as vegetables, meat, seafood, grain, cooking oils and dairy goods." If this is true within China, then it should also be true in foreign markets--- and a series of scandals involving toxic chemicals and other fillers in food products around the world confirm this. Yet, Chinese agricultural exports continue to increase, driven by their low prices.

The same is true in the pharmaceutical industry. There's been movement (again unexpected) of much of that industry from the United States to China since Beijing was allowed to join the World Trade Organization (a decision I opposed). This shift was motivated by the desire to cut costs by using cheap Chinese labor and by avoiding expensive regulation. This opened the door not only to lower quality output, but made it easier for counterfeiters to infiltrate supply chains. Drugs with weak dosages or no active ingredients at all endanger public health and discredit treatment programs.

Fake drugs undermine U.S. efforts to treat illnesses in developing countries. For example, the State Dept. has requested $650 million in the 2014 budget to fight malaria in developing countries. Yet, half the anti-malarial drugs on the markets in Southeast Asia and Africa have been found to be counterfeit. And most of these fake drugs come from China.

Fakes also threatened the campaign against diabetes and other significant and debilitating diseases.

Besides the global health, safety and security threats created by unscrupulous Chinese business practices and the corrupt lack of supervision by Chinese authorities, there is a competitive issue as well. American farmers are the most productive in the world and are held to rigorous standards. The same is true of the American pharmaceutical industry which creates the world's most advanced medicines. Yet, if U.S. exports are defeated in the marketplace on the basis of lower prices stemming from illicit cost cutting, then American producers, as well as our entire economy suffers.

Counterfeit products are often sold under the brand name of legitimate products such as Pfizer, Lipitor, Ambien and Xanax. Indeed, there is hardly an American company that has not been victimized by this Chinese larceny. And when the product does not work the brand is held responsible. This can slander the name of an American company and of the United States itself--- not to mention injure or kill those using the product.

Are there measures we can take---or persuade China to take, to safeguard consumers from dangerous exports; or should we just ban such goods from the market as inherently unsafe? The production and distribution of such critical goods as food and medicine, upon which life itself depends, cannot be trusted unless there is integrity throughout the manufacturing and supply chains. We have gathered a panel of experts to help us decide what our policy options are:

Mr. ROHRABACHER. With that, Mr. Keating, would you have an opening statement?

Mr. KEATING. Thank you, Mr. Chairman, and thank you for holding today's hearing. From tires to toothpaste to toys, Chinese imports account for more than 50 percent of the recalls announced by the Consumer Product Safety Commission. And China's monetary policies do not make it any easier for safer, American-made products to compete with their cheaper Chinese counterparts. Ultimately China's policies affect the safety of our children, our parents, grandparents, and pets here at home.

Increasingly, the conversation in Congress has turned to China as a rising super power that is increasingly investing in emerging markets worldwide, but the fact of the matter is that China still lacks the necessary governmental institutions based in rule of law, transparency, and accountability to be able to regulate its own products. Further, these institutional weaknesses extend to the realm of human rights abuses and media repression within China.

During the 2008 Olympic games in China, an official ban on reporting "all food safety issues" banned media from reporting on at least 20 dairy firms that were selling milk products that contained the chemical melamine. That coverup contributed to the deaths of six children and the illnesses among 300,000 others. And when Chinese officials attempted to enforce regulations which they have been doing as of late, their institutional weaknesses come back to haunt them. Just this year, in response to a campaign to crack down on marketing sick pigs in China, the Ministry of Public Security has been raiding farms, arresting violators, and then confiscating unsafe pork meat.

According to the Council on Foreign Relations during the celebration of the Lunar Chinese New York this year, the police stepped up efforts to rid the market of tainted pork meat. However, in absence of collaboration from other departments, these well-intended efforts led to over 6,000 unmarketable dead pigs being dumped into a local river. Thousands of carcasses were discovered floating in the Huangpu River which supplies drinking water to Shanghai's 23 million residents. The domestic implications for this huge and incredibly concerning practice are yet to be fully understood.

There are international implications as well. According to the same Council on Foreign Relations report, in 2011 alone China produced more than 50 million metric tons of pork accounting for nearly half the world-wide pork production. And unfortunately, we can easily list other instances like this throughout China as well as one recall after another for Chinese products in our own country here at home. For this reason, and the fact that China has been extending operations into developing regions of the world with even weaker standards, I do agree with you that China's unsafe products have the potential to become an even more widespread threat to global health and global safety.

I hope that today's hearing will shed some light as to why and which way we can proceed as a country to really protect our consumers at home and protect consumers throughout the world. I welcome our witnesses and look forward to their testimonies. And with that, thank you, Mr. Chairman, I yield back.

Mr. ROHRABACHER. Thank you for that very provocative opening statement. It gives new meaning to sweet and sour pork you might say. I now recognize Steve Stockman, the outspoken member of our committee from Texas.

Mr. STOCKMAN. Thank you, Mr. Chairman. I am glad you put this hearing together. We have in our district, rice, catfish, and pharmaceuticals. You can trust ours, and our labeling. And someone who buys organic food and purchases organic food, and now finds that the society which professes to be socialist and caring, and not driven by greed, is actually driven by greed and mislabels organic food and other products is very Orwellian, I guess, to say the least. I thank you for holding these hearings. I am looking forward to the testimonies of our guests today. Thank you.

Mr. ROHRABACHER. Thank you very much. It is ironic that for all of these years, the communists were talking about how horrible free enterprise and capitalism is and here they have turned their back on their own country while they still have a government that claims allegiance to Marx and Lenin and they just turned their back on this most predatory and awful example of irresponsibility in the name of making a profit.

Now today we have four witnesses and what I am going to do is introduce all four now and then we will each have about 5 minutes to give your presentation. Anything more than that we will be happy to put in the record and then we will have some questions and answers. First, we have William Triplett. He is an author and consultant with great experience with China. You have been a consultant for four decades now. Mr. Triplett began his professional career with the American intelligence community working China issues overseas. Later, he was the Deputy Assistant U.S. Trade Representative for the East-West meaning China during the first Reagan administration. He served for 9 years on the staff of the Senate Foreign Relations Committee reaching the post of chief Republican counsel to the committee. His most recent—he has several books—is Bowing To Beijing, published last year and he is a frequent contributor to newspapers and professional journals.

We also have with us Patty Lovera and she is assistant director of the nonprofit Food & Water Watch where she coordinates the organization's food policy program. She has a bachelor's degree in environmental science and a master's degree in environmental policy from the University of Michigan. Before joining the Food & Water Watch, she was a deputy director of the Energy and Environment Program at Public Citizen and a researcher at the Center for Health, Environment, and Justice.

We have with us also Mark Kastel and is co-founder of The Cornucopia Institute, a foreign policy research group based in Wisconsin and director of its Organic Integrity Project. For almost 20 years prior to the launch of this institute, he was president of M.A. Kastel and Associates, a professional practice that include political consulting, lobbying, business development, and benefitting family scale farmers.

Finally, Sophie Richardson is the China director at the Human Rights Watch, a graduate of the University of Virginia, the Hopkins-Nanjing Program and Oberlin College. Dr. Richardson is the author of numerous articles on domestic Chinese political reform, democratization and human rights in Cambodia, China, Indonesia, Hong Kong and the Philippines and Vietnam. Her book, ''China, Cambodia, and the Five Principles of Peaceful Coexistence'' was published by Columbia University Press and is an in-depth examination of China's foreign policy since the 1954 Geneva Conference. With that said, we have our witnesses with us today and we will start with Mr. Kastel.

STATEMENT OF MR. MARK KASTEL, CO–FOUNDER, THE CORNUCOPIA INSTITUTE

Mr. KASTEL. Thank you, Mr. Chairman. My name is Mark Alan Kastel. I am the co-director and act as senior farm policy analyst at The Cornucopia Institute. We are based in Cornucopia, Wisconsin.

Cornucopia is a tax-exempt farm policy research group. We act as an organic industry watchdog.

We have long been concerned about the propriety of organic commodities and finished products being imported into the United States from China.

Mr. Chairman, many in this country, for good reason, based on history, do not trust the Chinese to supply ingredients for our dog and our cat food. Why should we trust these Chinese exporters with food that we are feeding our children and our families?

Besides any specific concerns and evidence regarding organics, this is a country with endemic levels of commercial fraud whether in intellectual property, the counterfeiting of name-brand consumer products, or being engaged in industrial espionage.

The organic marketplace was founded as an ethical alternative for consumers seeking safer and more nutritious food to serve their families. We looked at Chinese organics as part of our research and investigation in preparing our report, ''Behind the Bean.'' We found that although there were many exemplary U.S. manufacturers, the majority of the participants in the organic soy industry were shifting to Chinese organic imports. And in particular, we highlighted Dean Foods' WhiteWave Division which manufactures the market-leader, Silk soy milk. They threw U.S. organic producers under the bus by asking them to match cheaper Chinese prices which they were unable to do.

In Cornucopia's 2009 Soy Food Report, we estimated that as much as half of all organic soybeans being sold in the United States came from overseas, primarily China. It is probably higher now.

We were told by domestic soybean buyers and processors of food-grade soybeans that brokers came to them with a choice. They had A beans and B beans. What is the difference? The brokers told us that the A beans were from farms and suppliers they had personally visited in China and they could vouch for the authenticity of the product. And the B beans? Well, the brokers had a piece of paper, a certification document that says they are organic. And they are cheaper.

Most commonly we found that the ones that got purchased were the B beans.

In February 2011, the USDA's National Organic Program started informing the public of fraudulent organic certificates, these pieces of paper that I referenced. They found that of 22 fraudulent organic certificates since that point in time, 9 were from China. The next highest country had only three from India where we are also seeing an exponential increase in organic imports.

And whether it is melamine contaminating processed food, rat meat masquerading as lamb, or dead hogs floating down that river you referenced, we don't trust—the Chinese don't trust the food they are producing. Why should we?

The USDA and FDA inspectors are only examining as referenced 1–2 percent of all food that reaches U.S. ports. And what are they finding? A disproportionate number of serious problems from China: Adulteration, unapproved chemicals, dyes, pesticides, and outright fraud, fake food.

The remaining 98 percent that is not inspected, well, that might be on your table tonight for dinner or at the restaurant you might be enjoying.

The largest organic farmer cooperative in this country, Organic Valley, is now exporting packaged milk to China. You can understand why a growing, affluent cross section of the Chinese populace is buying imported U.S. commodities. What do they know that many in the United States don't know about the safety of Chinese food?

The farmers I work for have names and they have a story and they have a background and they are competing with these pieces of paper. Organics continue to grow even in this tight economy, but for the first time we are seeing a net loss in the number of organic farmers in the Midwest and Rocky Mountain States and we are losing thousands of acres of farmland. We can't compete with the Chinese without a level playing field in terms of aggressive certification and enforcement of organic law.

In conclusion, the Cornucopia Institute welcomes congressional pressure on the FDA and USDA to fulfill their mandates, to protect domestic farmers, organic consumers and all consumers from the dangerous fraud in the importation of food from China, India, former Soviet bloc states, or any other country exporting poison to our shores and we hope that you folks will adequately augment their budget and watchdog them to make sure they are carrying out their missions. Thank you very much, Mr. Chairman.

[The prepared statement of Mr. Kastel follows:]

Testimony of:

Mark Alan Kastel
Codirector and Senior Farm Policy Analyst

The Cornucopia Institute

Before:

House Committee on Foreign Affairs
Subcommittee on Europe, Eurasia and Emerging Threats

May 8, 2013

CORNUCOPIA

INSTITUTE

Thank you, Mr. Chairman.

My name is Mark Alan Kastel. I'm the Codirector and act as senior farm policy analyst at The Cornucopia Institute. We are based in Cornucopia, Wisconsin.

The Cornucopia Institute is a tax-exempt farm policy research group. We act as an organic industry watchdog.

We have long been concerned about the propriety of organic commodities and finished products being imported to the United States from China.

Mr. Chairman, many in this country, for good reason, based on history, do not trust the Chinese to supply ingredients <u>for our dog and cat food</u>. Why should we trust Chinese exporters for the food that we are feeding our children and families?

Besides for any specific concerns and evidence regarding organics, this is a country with endemic levels of commercial fraud whether in intellectual property, the counterfeiting of name-brand consumer products, or being engaged in industrial espionage.

The organic marketplace was founded as an ethical alternative for consumers seeking safer and more nutritious food to serve their families. In addition, we know from focus group work that the reason there is such low price resistance to the premiums paid for organic food is that consumers don't think they are <u>just</u> selfishly protecting their families. They believe that the investment also pays dividends for society in supporting a different kind of environmental ethic, a more humane animal husbandry model .... and economic justice for the people who produce our food.

In many ways Chinese imports undermine the foundational precepts that the organic movement was founded upon.

We first investigated Chinese organics as part of our research and investigation in preparing our report *Behind the Bean — the Heroes and Charlatans of the Natural and Organic Soy Foods Industry.*

We found that although there were many exemplary U.S. manufacturers, like Clinton, Michigan-based Eden Foods, that has direct relationships with farmers in the United States growing organic soybeans, the majority of the participants in the organic soy industry were shifting to Chinese organic imports.

In particular we highlighted Dean Foods' WhiteWave division, which manufactures the market-leader, Silk soy "milk." (I use the quotation marks because the hard-working dairy farmers I work with find calling crushed soybeans and water "milk" objectionable.)

At a time of rapid industry growth, instead of paying U.S. farmer cooperatives the market rate for certified organic soybeans, they threw U.S. organic producers under the bus by asking them to match cheaper Chinese prices (which they were unable to do). The company has since shifted most of their products over to conventional soybeans.

But the damage was done. And it continues to be done in the marketplace. In Cornucopia's 2009 soy foods report, we estimated that as much as half of organic soybeans used in the U.S. came from overseas, primarily China—it's probably higher now.

We are told by domestic soybean buyers and processors of food-grade soybeans that brokers come to them with a choice. They have "A-beans" and "B-beans."

What's the difference? The brokers tell them that the A-beans are from farms and suppliers that they have personally visited in China and they can vouch for the authenticity of the product. And the B-beans? Well, the brokers have a piece of paper, a certification document, that says they're organic. And they're cheaper. Most commonly, they're the ones that get purchased.

In February 2011, the USDA's National Organic Program started informing the public of fraudulent organic certificates, those "pieces of paper" I just referred to. They have found 22 fraudulent organic certificates, and nine were from China. The next highest country had only three: that was India, where we are also seeing an exponential increase in organic imports.

And whether it's melamine contaminating processed food, rat meat masquerading as lamb, or dead hogs floating down rivers supplying the drinking water, many Chinese consumers don't trust their domestically produced food. Why should we?

USDA and FDA inspectors are only examining 1%-2% of all the food that reaches U.S. ports. And what are they finding? A disproportionate number of serious problems with exports from China including adulteration with unapproved chemicals, dyes, pesticides and outright fraud (fake food).

What of the remaining 98% of Chinese exports? They might very well be on your table tonight either at home or at a restaurant.

The largest farmer-owned organic cooperative in this country, Organic Valley, based in Wisconsin, is now exporting packaged milk to China. This doesn't make any more ecological sense than importing frozen Chinese vegetables to America. But you can understand why a growing, more affluent cross-section of the Chinese populace is stripping the store shelves bare in Europe and Australia of infant formula, and buying imported U.S. organics. What do they know that many in the United States don't about the safety of Chinese-grown commodities?

Because of the restricted nature of doing business in China, U.S. certifiers are unable to independently inspect farms and assure compliance to the USDA organic food and agriculture standards that are required for export to the U.S. Inspections are conducted by foreign-owned certification agencies accredited by the USDA. But even they cannot freely operate in the country without Chinese government oversight.

These imports should not be allowed to reach our shore until and unless we have a system in place to assure consumers they are getting what they pay for. Just like U.S. grown organic commodities, the safety of these products must be rigorously overseen by independent inspectors.

The farmers I work for have names. They have photographs of their farms. And they would welcome members of this committee, or the organic public, for a visit any time. They are not just selling soybeans. They are selling the story behind their beans. They are competing with anonymous Chinese commodities backed by pieces of paper of questionable authenticity.

Organics continue to grow, even in this tight economy. But for the first time we are seeing a net loss in the number of organic farmers in the Midwest and Rocky Mountain states, and we are losing thousands of acres of farmland. We cannot compete with the Chinese without a level playing field in terms of aggressive certification and enforcement of organic law.

The Cornucopia Institute welcomes congressional pressure on the FDA and the USDA to fulfill their mandates to protect domestic farmers, organic consumers, and <u>all consumers</u>, from dangerous fraud in the importation of food from China, India, former Soviet bloc states, or any other country exporting poison to our shores. And we hope you will adequately augment their budgets while holding them responsible for carrying out their missions.

Thank you.

Mr. ROHRABACHER. Thank you very much. That was very thoughtful. We will have some questions.

Mr. Triplett.

STATEMENT OF MR. WILLIAM TRIPLETT II, AUTHOR AND CONSULTANT (FORMER CHIEF REPUBLICAN COUNSEL, SENATE COMMITTEE ON FOREIGN RELATIONS)

Mr. TRIPLETT. Good afternoon, Mr. Chairman, and Distinguished Ranking Member. I am William C. Triplett II, and with the committee's permission I would like my prepared statement put in the record and I will speak just briefly off the cuff.

Mr. ROHRABACHER. Certainly with no objection. Thank you.

Mr. TRIPLETT. Last week, they had a lot of fun with the rat meat story that was in the newspaper and on headlines and so forth. Chinese Supreme Court Judge was quoted, ''The situation is really gray and has indeed caused great harm to the people.'' Certainly, he is right. And he is talking about the Chinese people, but the obvious problem is that that stuff comes to us, too.

There is three ways we can look at it. One is the adulterated food issue. The second one is their deficient health system. And the third one which I would like to talk about a little bit is pollution for thee, but not for me. One of the things we have known for a long time is that the Chinese cadres had their own farms. They don't trust the food and so forth and so on. That is number one. The farmers themselves don't trust their own food. They won't eat what they produce, so they ship it to another province. Rich people are leaving the country and in the exit interviews they are being asked why are you leaving and the answer is because of food safety and so forth and so on. One of the other things is Chinese communist officials even have special filters on the buildings that they work in so that they don't have to breathe the foul air.

Now the issue of is this becoming our problem, I have a graph in the prepared statement that shows that in the last 3 years, Chinese agricultural imports are going up by about $½ billion a year. That is the first graph. And of course, imports of poultry are going up at an even higher rate.

The question is can the Chinese solve the problem on their own? I don't think that I know anybody who studies this closely who really thinks the Chinese can handle it themselves. I think the system is simply too corrupt and I think we are going to hear that from several of the witnesses today and so forth and so on.

I would like to turn to what the Congress and the committee can do about it. First and foremost, I want to commend the committee for holding this hearing. That is the alpha, if you will, of the alpha and omega of solutions because without this kind of a hearing, then this issue will get lost with the other issues.

The second end of the issue is this is the omega. And that is when China becomes a democratic country, then the people will demand safe food and safe food for them will then ultimately mean safe food for us. So we are between these two ends. The question is what to do in the middle?

I have a lot of experience, as the chairman well knows, in arms smuggling of Chinese to terrorist countries and groups and so forth and so on. Smuggling is a real big deal. I would hope the committee would encourage the usual suspects to find out basically who is involved, who are the names, who are the corrupt officials and so forth and so on who are engaged in this food safety business. That is the first thing. Let us take names.

The second thing is I think we need to change the terms of reference. New York Times today had a big story about how we need $3 billion more for food inspection. I am generally sympathetic with that, but on the other hand if you look at the honey case, I am not sure how much money would be sufficient and I think the onus should go the other direction and that is the Chinese would basically guarantee that their food is safe.

The other thing is a question of draconian punishments. Congress has a history of imposing draconian punishments, the Toshiba case being the most famous example. And also this committee has jurisdiction over the International Emergency Economic Powers Act.

Third, I have included something called the strategic policy framework which was circulated in the last Congress and is essentially a way to organized looking at Chinese issues from a comprehensive standpoint. So if you put the three together, take names, that is number one. Number two is change the terms of reference. Number three, begin to talk about really draconian measures against some of the people who are engaged in this and then do this all in a comprehensive way. I think that would be the best of my suggestions. Thank you very much for the opportunity to speak.

[The prepared statement of Mr. Triplett follows:]

TESTIMONY FOR THE HOUSE COMMITTEE ON FOREIGN AFFAIRS

Subcommittee on Europe, Eurasia and Emerging Threats

The Threat of China's Unsafe Consumables

May 8, 2013

William C. Triplett, II

Mr. Chairman and distinguished Members, thank you for the opportunity to appear here today.

Does China face a serious food safety crisis?

Inserting the words "China food safety" into the Internet leads to over 155 million hits, none of them laudatory so far as a brief examination can tell. As a Seattle Times reporter noted recently, "It's no secret that China has a tainted food problem." [i] And so it does. Therefore it is no wonder that Russia's top health official this spring advised Russian citizens against visiting China and announced that he is considering restrictions on agricultural imports from China. [ii] A problem evolves into a crisis when major newspapers begin leading with, "Chinese pupils die after drinking yoghurt [yogurt] laced with rat poison", as London's *Guardian* headlined last week. [iii]

How is China's food safety crisis defined?

Adulteration-

This is essentially the tainted food aspect. Hundreds of cases of tainted or poisoned food originating in China had been reported even before the rat-meat-for-mutton story hit the international headlines last week. Even as the Chinese Government was announcing the rat meat story it reminded readers some of the more notorious cases:

*liquor made with industrial alcohol [five dead]

*pork adulterated with clenbuterol

*melamine-laced infant formula [six dead and 300,000 injured]

*toxic gelatin for medicine capsules [iv]

As a Chinese Supreme Court Judge was quoted, "The situation is really grave and has indeed caused great harm to the people." [v]

China's deficient and dangerous health system-

On the deficiency side is the issue of the Chinese health system's belated response to the current bird flu [H7N9] strain. At least 27 people have died through early May and there is no indication that China's health authorities are any closer to getting it under control. The Center for Disease Control is very concerned about possible "mutations" that would give it a person-to-person threat [vi] and there is additional concern that politics played a role in Chinese authorities holding back news of how widespread the epidemic really is [vii].

On a more dangerous note, it now appears that Chinese virus scientists are deliberately making new strains of the virus in the laboratory. Lord May of Oxford, a former top British scientist, has declared this practice "appalling irresponsibility" and accused the Chinese research team of being "driven by blind ambition". [viii] This may be a case where Hollywood's disaster movie producers were ahead of the curve.

Pollution for thee but not for me.

In April public radio's "Marketplace" did an excellent three-part series entitled, "China's Toxic Farms". [ix] Soil, water and air pollution is taking an enormous toll on the Chinese people who eat, drink and breathe the results of China's industrial practices. Looking at this and other reporting reveals the following:

*Many Chinese farms are so damaged from industrial pollution that the farmers won't eat their own products. They ship it out to other provinces. [x]

*The long-time system of secret organic farms just for Chinese Communist Party officials and the newly rich continues, in one case disguised as a "country club". [xi]

    *Chinese Communist Party officials even have special air filters for their offices and residences so they won't breathe the foul air. [xii]

    *China's newly rich are making plans to leave the country and they list "food safety" as one of the driving issues.[xiii]

    *Those with enough money in China are increasingly turning to food imports from other countries because they don't trust the domestic product. [xiv]

    One amusing case is that of Dulwich College in Beijing, an international high school based on the British model. A visit to their website reveals a large mound on the left hand side. It's a climate-controlled dome which covers basketball courts and other outdoor recreational facilities. When the pollution in Beijing is too bad for the children to be out on their regular playgrounds, they can exercise here, a benefit denied the Chinese people for their children.[xv]

Is China's food safety crisis now becoming our problem?

    In the summer of 1982 the Chinese began to show off their economic plans for South China to Americans. So, as Deputy Assistant United States Trade Representative in charge of China trade, I went to a little fishing village just across the border from Hong Kong. With the exception of bare-bulb electric lights, the little village looked like it had not changed in hundreds of years but the officials were very optimistic declaring that "such and such" will be built in this place and something else would be over there, and so on. I was polite but privately skeptical, pretty much a universal American view in those days.

    The little fishing village turned out to be the boom-town exporting zone known as Shenzhen and the Chinese have replicated that success in many parts of the country. In 1982 China's trade with the non-socialist world was in the neighborhood of $40 billion. Now, it's well over a trillion dollars.

    This graph based on USDA figures shows Total Agricultural Imports from China for the past three years:

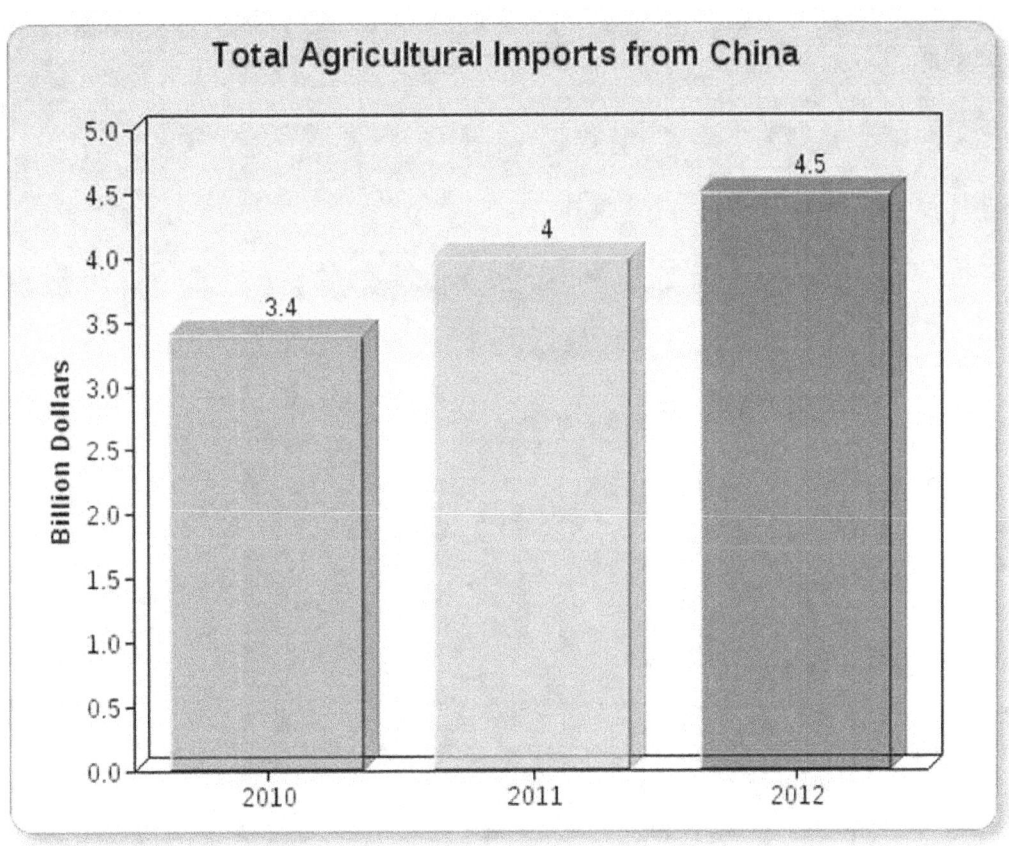

Even in recent difficult economic times, agriculture imports from China are rising about half a billion dollars per year.

And this graph shows US poultry imports from China, again based on USDA figures:

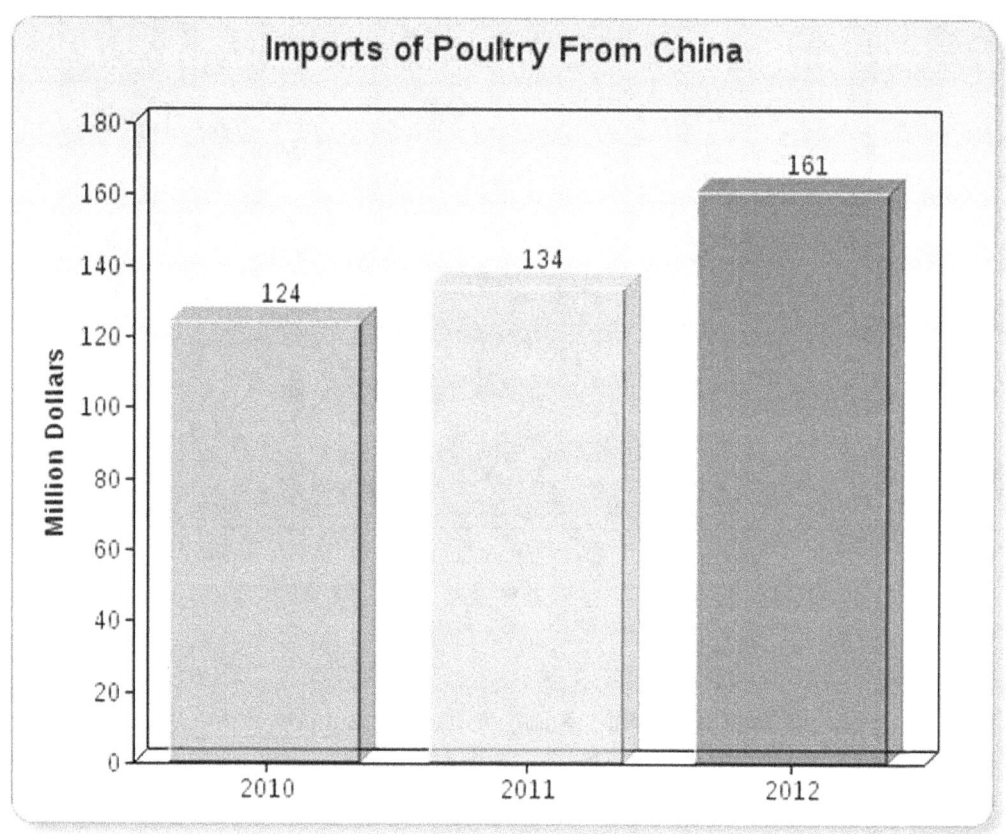

Imports of Poultry From China

Here we are looking at an increasing rate of increase as poultry imports went up by $10 million from 2010 to 2011 and $27 million from 2011 to 2012.

In 2011, "Food and Water Watch" produced an excellent monograph entitled "A Decade of Dangerous Food Imports from China". Two years later, it appears the problem is worse rather than better. Last fall thousands of German children fell ill after eating Chinese strawberries served to them in their school cafeterias.[xvi] And just last month the FDA revealed that thanks to toxic battery recycling operations, rice imported from China showed lead levels 60 times above the recommended safe levels for children.[xvii]

One of the particular problems of dealing with toxic food imports from China is illustrated by the honey case. The FDA and others got onto the Chinese honey issue quite a while ago. The Department of Justice even raided some facilities but the consensus is that through a sophisticated international smuggling network, the Chinese honey producers have pretty well defeated all efforts to control them.[xviii]

So the short answer, is "Yes, the Chinese food safety crisis is about to become our problem as well."

Can the Chinese solve the problem on their own?

Last Friday the Chinese Ministry of Public Safety and the Chinese press announced a major crackdown on food safety issues. Numbers were rolled out to show a big increase in criminal cases and successful prosecutions. They threw out the rat meat story to gain public and international attention.

But how real was this?

Dr. June Teufel Dreyer teaches Chinese Politics at the University of Miami and her textbook, The Chinese Political System, now in its eighth printing, is the standard in the area. When asked about this, she responded, "Corruption is the glue of China's state-sponsored and state-dependent capitalism." [xix]

After looking at the Chinese Communist Party for over four decades, I conclude that the system is just too corrupt to institute any real reform that would impact the Chinese people or us in any meaningful way.

Here is just one example: Levels of soil pollution in China, critical to any discussion of food safety, are a state secret and people who reveal state secrets go to jail[xx].

As another example, on the very day last week that one arm of the Chinese Communist Party was patting itself on the back for its efforts to control food safety issues, another arm was blocking a series of sensitive words on pollution from the Chinese internet.[xxi]

What can be done?

First and foremost, the Chairman is to be commended for shining the light on this obviously emerging threat to the American people. Without this hearing, the issue would fall away until the real crisis comes. In fact, I hope the Committee can expand the scope of its consideration to include pharmaceuticals and perhaps cosmetics.

Second, as a practical matter, the only long term solution to this or any other China-related problem is for China to become a democratic country. A free press and officials accountable to the people will ensure that safe food, water and air are basic human rights and not just for the rich. If Chinese food is safe at home, we can have some confidence that what they send us will also be safe. I know the Chairman has been deeply engaged in promoting democracy and human rights in China for a long time and hope that others will join him.

Third, we lack some basic data. In the case of Chinese arms sales to rogue regimes, we've known the cast of characters for decades but in the case of food safety, we don't really know who in China prospers from having the system continue as it is. The Committee could task the relevant agencies to name some names and thus create a data base.

Fourth, it's time to change the terms of reference. The FDA inspects perhaps 1-2% of Chinese food exports to the United States. Given the experience of the honey case, I don't think there is anywhere near enough taxpayer's money to play whack-a-mole with the Chinese toxic exporters around the Pacific that would make any real difference. Nor should we. Why should the taxpayers have to pay for Chinese companies to make lucrative exports to us? Shouldn't the Chinese Government be guaranteeing the fitness of its very profitable exports? We could be in the absurd position of borrowing money from China to protect ourselves from Chinese poisoned food.

Fifth, the Congress should be prepared to enforce draconian punishments in the event of a major food safety event. Twenty-five years ago the Japanese industrial firm, Toshiba, thought restrictions on sensitive military technology exports to the then-Soviet Union didn't apply to them. Congress stepped in, it cost the company half a billion dollars in lost trade with the United States but the problem was solved. Japan greatly upgraded its export regulations and is no longer a conduit for military technology to the wrong hands. The Congress has already in place the International Emergency Economic Powers Act, legislation which is under the jurisdiction of this Committee. President Obama used IEEPA in 2010 to fine a major British bank $300 million for trading with Iran[xxii]. Certainly we can do as much with our children's health.

Sixth, I would like to recommend that the "strategic policy framework for U. S. relations with the People's Republic of China" be re-considered. It circulated in the previous Congress but did not advance due to the press of time. It offers a comprehensive way forward to deal with the problems we now face dealing with China on an ad hoc basis. I have attached a copy of the original proposal.

Finally, this thought. Two Nobel Peace Prize winners were born within the borders of what is now the People's Republic of China. One is in exile and the other one is in jail. Ours is President of the United States. It is this dichotomy that explains the fundamental problem of dealing with Beijing on food safety, Tibet, arms smuggling to rogue regimes or any of the other US-China issues. It also points to the difficulties we will have resolving them in the era before China becomes a democratic country.

---

[i] "Questions Remain About Organic Foods Grown in China", *Seattle Times*, January 10, 2011

[ii] 'Russians should not visit China-Top Public Health Official", *RIA Novosti,* May 3, 2013

[iii] "Chinese Pupils Die after drinking Yoghurt Laced with Rat Poison", *Guardian,* May 3, 2013

[iv] China Vows Harsher Punishment of food-related crimes", *Xinhua,* May 3, 2013

[v] "Rat Meat Sold as Lamb in Latest China Food Scandal", *AP,* May 3, 2013

[vi] "New Bird Flu Well-adapted to Infect People", *CNN,* April 12, 2013

[vii] "China's Actions in Flu Cases Draw Critics", *The New York Times,* April 10, 2013

[viii] "'Appalling Irresponsibility'", *The Independent* [London], May 2, 2013

[ix] http:www.marketplace.org/world/china's-toxic-harvest

[x] ibid

[xi] "In China, What you Eat Tells Who You Are", *Los Angeles Times,* September 16, 2011

[xii] "The Privileges of China's Elite Include Purified Air", *New York Times,* November 4, 2011

[xiii] "Why China's Rich Want to Leave", *The Atlantic,* April 11, 2013

[xiv] Marketplace op. cit

[xv] "Why Leave Job in Beijing? To Breath", *Wall Street Journal,* April 13, 2013

[xvi] "'You get what you pay for', The Hidden Price of Food from China", *Spiegel,* October 17, 2012

[xvii] "Thanks to Recycled Batteries", *Daily Mail* [London], April 11, 2013

[xviii] "Asian Honey, Banned in Europe, is Flooding U. S. Grocery Shelves", *Food Safety News,* August 15, 2011

[xix] With permission

[xx] "Report on Mainland China's Soil pollution a 'state secret'", *South China Morning Post* [Hong Kong], February 26, 2013

[xxi] Withheld to protect source

[xxii] Press Release, US Department of Justice, August 18, 2010

H.Res. _____ U.S. RELATIONS WITH CHINA

Setting forth a strategic policy framework for U.S. relations with the People's Republic of China to guide matters before the House of Representatives.

Whereas

Relations between the United States and China will be key to Americans' peace and prosperity for decades to come, but successive U.S. administrations have failed to provide a guiding strategy or framework for U.S. policy toward China, inviting conflicting and internally contradictory policy pursuits;

There is a time-honored bond of friendship between the American and Chinese peoples, but the Government of China has continued to oppress the people of China by denying basic human rights, such as freedom of speech and religion, and suppressing minority groups;

The PRC has become a formidable economic power and a significant trading partner to the betterment of American consumers and businesses who enjoy access to decent quality, low-cost Chinese goods, but the PRC has repeatedly violated WTO rules and U.S. export controls laws, engaged in industrial and cyber espionage, and infringed U.S. patent and other intellectual property rights;

The U.S. has a historic commitment to freedom of the seas, strategic partnerships with Japan and Taiwan, strong defense alliances and cooperation with regional allies, but the PRC is pursuing a rapid military buildup that challenges U.S. defense capabilities and the stability and security of friends and allies in East Asia and the Pacific.

Successive U.S. administrations have worked to achieve more transparency and confidence in China's relationship with the U.S. and Chinese activities worldwide, but China continues to regard the United States as its principal strategic adversary and to expand its military, intelligence and economic reach globally, including a significant intelligence presence within the United States.

Therefore be it Resolved, that House of Representatives shall measure such bills and resolutions as may be considered by this Body or its Committees of jurisdiction concerning or affecting U.S. relations with China against these guiding strategic U.S. objectives:

> To sustain and deploy clear and unambiguous defense and intelligence capabilities to resist any resort to force or other forms of coercion that would jeopardize the peace and stability of the Asia/Pacific region or the security of U.S. friends and allies;

> To exert internal pressure on the Chinese government to support liberalization, transparency, democratization and human rights;

> To engage with the Chinese government to eliminate, on the basis of strict reciprocity, outstanding disagreements;

> To convey clearly to Beijing that responsible behavior on their part will create the possibility for a genuine partnership to our mutual advantage, while any unacceptable behavior will incur costs that would outweigh any gains;

> To prevent the transfer of technology, intellectual property or equipment that would make a substantial contribution to Chinese military capability; and

> To ensure a robust economy and self-sufficiency at home as the surest means of providing leverage to deal with China on all fronts.

Resolved further, that any and all Authorization or Appropriations Bills reported to the Full House for consideration shall be accompanied by a Report setting forth their compliance with these principles.

Mr. Rohrabacher. And Ms. Lovera

STATEMENT OF MS. PATTY LOVERA, ASSISTANT DIRECTOR, FOOD & WATER WATCH

Ms. Lovera. Good afternoon. My name is Patty Lovera and I am the assistant director of Food & Water Watch. We are a nonprofit consumer advocacy organization and we appreciate the opportunity to present testimony on this important topic.

As we have discussed, the United States is increasingly reliant on imported food and China is in the position as the world's largest agricultural economy to send us a lot of the food that we are importing. We import over 1 billion pounds of fruits and vegetables from China every year and over 1 billion pounds of fish and seafood. For some products, like apple juice and garlic, China has already started to replace domestic production of crops that we have traditionally grown here. And it is not just fresh produce or even fruits and vegetables and seafood. We are increasingly bringing in processed foods and the ingredients that we use in processed foods.

In 2010, we imported 81 million pounds of spices and 41 million pounds of pasta and baked goods from China.

I have included some charts with a lot more data on these trends in the written testimony that I have submitted.

Food safety problems in China have obviously been making headlines for a while. We spoke already about contamination of foods with melamine. The one point I will add to the melamine story is why melamine was in the food. So melamine is an ingredient in plastics and it has been intentionally added to these food products to try to artificially increase the nitrogen contents in those foods, to attempt to beat laboratory tests for protein levels. So this was not an accidental contamination. This was intentional adulterated with an economic motive, to try to beat laboratory tests.

So despite very public efforts in recent years by the Chinese Government to crack down on food safety problems, it is kind of a continual feed of bad news from the food safety front from China. We have heard a lot of these examples already.

I do want to spend a minute talking about what our Government is doing in terms of protecting U.S. consumers with our oversight of these imports. We have already heard that the FDA can inspect less than 2 percent of imported produce, processed food, and seafood which we think almost guarantees that some unsafe Chinese products are going to make their way on to our store shelves.

The FDA opened its first office in China in 2008. However, the few FDA inspectors in China are overwhelmed by the sheer size of the nation's food production including an estimated 1 million food processing companies. In Fiscal Year 2012, FDA conducted ten inspections of food facilities in China.

When it comes to meat and poultry imports, that is the responsibility of the Department of Agriculture. And we are not yet importing meat and poultry for human consumption from China, but that process is underway and we are concerned about the way that USDA is regulating imports of these products from other countries and what that will mean if China does get approved. The USDA recently announced in 2009 that it made a major change to its oversight of imports by ending annual in-depth audit visits it would make to exporting countries. Now they are relying on a self-reporting tool for countries as a substitute. And that means they are going to do those audit visits every 3 years instead of annually. So if we reach a point and the process is ongoing now where China gets approved as equivalent to send processed chicken products here, we worry that that is the process the USDA will use and it is clearly not sufficient.

Just a few recommendations that we would have about what we can be doing on the U.S. front to protect consumers from this situation? We think in the big picture it is really important to think about that this is not an unforeseeable outcome. This is not an accident. We are combining trade policy that makes the U.S. more and more reliant on importing food with a food safety regulatory system that is not up to the job of dealing with that rising tide of imports. So in addition to examining our trade policy, we think we also need to really take a hard look at the changes we need to make to our food safety programs.

So specifically, we think the USDA should conduct an entirely new investigation before allowing Chinese poultry products to be exported to the United States. If these imports are approved, USDA should permanently assign inspection personnel to China so that the exporting plants receive regular visits by USDA inspectors.

When it comes to the FDA, they need the resources to conduct more inspections in food facilities in China rather than relying on third party certifications of the safety practices used by exporting firms. So this is a model that is being proposed under new food safety legislation that would make the FDA very reliant on using third parties to verify that food from other countries is safe. We don't think that is adequate for U.S. consumers. It is the government's job to do these safety inspections. So we are quite concerned about that.

And then finally, consumers do have one tool right now to protect themselves which is country of origin labeling which is mandatory, thanks to Federal law. It covers meat, seafood, fruits and vegetables and some nuts, but there are problems in the coverage of that labeling program because of the way that USDA has defined the word processed. The law says processed foods don't get a label. USDA wrote an incredibly broad definition of processed, so a lot of forms of these foods that should be covered are not required to have a label. So we think that USDA should change that definition so consumers get more coverage of the country of origin label. Thank you.

[The prepared statement of Ms. Lovera follows:]

Food & Water Watch • 1616 P St. NW, Suite 300 • Washington, DC 20036
T +202.683.2500 • F +202.683.2501 • www.foodandwaterwatch.org

Testimony before the
House Committee on Foreign Affairs
Subcommittee on Europe, Eurasia, and Emerging Threats

Hearing on
The Threat of China's Unsafe Consumables

May 8, 2013

Patty Lovera
Assistant Director
Food & Water Watch

My name is Patty Lovera, and I am the assistant director of Food & Water Watch, a nonprofit consumer advocacy organization. Thank you for the opportunity to present testimony on this important topic.

Introduction

The United States is increasingly reliant on imported food. The U.S. Government Accountability Office (GAO) reports that from 2000 through 2011, the percentage of food consumed in the United States that was imported rose from 9 percent to over 16 percent, and food imports increased by an average of 10 percent each year for seven years.[1] According to the U.S. Department of Agriculture's (USDA) Economic Research Service, the food groups with the highest share of imports are fresh fish and shellfish (85 percent in 2009) and fruits and nuts (38 percent in 2009).[2]

China is a growing supplier of the United State's food imports. China is the largest agricultural economy in the world and one of the biggest agricultural exporters.[3] It is the world's leading producer of many foods Americans eat: apples, tomatoes, peaches, potatoes, garlic, sweet potatoes, pears, peas — the list goes on and on.[4] It is also a leading producer of many of the inputs used to make processed food, for example ascorbic acid, or vitamin C, producing about 80 percent of the world supply.[5]

But the poorly controlled expansion of China's economy has often been fueled by excess pollution, treacherous working conditions, and dangerous foods and products that pose significant risks to consumers in China and worldwide. China's food manufacturers often found to cut corners and substitute dangerous ingredients to boost sales.

Food safety problems in China have been making headlines around the world for quite a while, especially after several rounds of publicity concerning contamination of foods with a chemical, normally used to make plastic, called melamine. The chemical has been intentionally added to different food products in China, usually to try to artificially increase the nitrogen content in attempt to pass tests for protein levels.

29

In 2007, the U.S. Food and Drug Administration (FDA) received reports of 17,000 pet illnesses, including 4,000 dog and cat deaths, believed to be the result of melamine contamination in imported Chinese gluten used to make pet food.[6] Sixty million packages of pet food were recalled in the United States.[7] The potential health impacts were not necessarily limited to pet food, however, because some of the melamine-contaminated pet food was redirected to hog farms. Thousands of hogs that ate the contaminated food were put to death in an effort to keep melamine-contaminated meat from entering the food supply.[8] But the FDA and USDA still allowed 56,000 hogs that ate melamine-tainted pet food to be processed into pork, which was then sold at supermarkets.[9]

By 2008, the FDA had identified melamine in imported wheat gluten and rice protein from China (used in pet food), prompting rejections of 44 percent and 32 percent of these products, respectively.[10] While the FDA stopped these shipments, pet food imports from China continued to rise and reached 79 million pounds in 2010.[11]

Pet food turned out to be only the tip of the melamine iceberg. Because melamine was widely used in China to adulterate dairy products such as milk powder, processed food products including candy, hot cocoa, flavored drinks and, most tragically, infant formula contained the chemical.[12] An infant formula scandal erupted just before the 2008 Beijing Olympics and ultimately an estimated 300,000 infants and children in China were sickened by melamine; more than 12,000 were hospitalized.[13] At least six children died.[14]

Melamine-tainted milk was also exported worldwide. The New Zealand-based food company Fonterra became caught up in the melamine scandal through a joint venture with the Chinese dairy company Sanlu that was implicated in the melamine crisis.[15] The scandal played out across the globe, ending up in the food supplies of companies including Mars, Unilever, Heinz, Cadbury and Yum! Brands, Inc. (which owns Pizza Hut, KFC, Taco Bell and other fast food chains).[16]

While the melamine crisis may be the most widely covered Chinese food safety scandal, unfortunately it was not an isolated incident. International media sources routinely cover food safety problems originating in China, ranging from widespread smuggling of products like honey to avoid tariffs and food safety restrictions,[17] mislabeled products "transshipped" through another country but produced in China,[18] and importing countries discovering violations of pesticide or other food safety regulations.

A 2013 report by a food industry analyst found that among reported food violations in Chinese products, the most frequent cause was pesticides, followed by pathogen contamination. The report cited 32 pesticides found in laboratory testing of Chinese foods, mostly in produce, fruit and spices and noted that "economically motivated adulteration" is a persistent issue in food production in China.[19]

These food safety problems have not gone unnoticed by consumers in the United States or China. After more than a decade of increased food imports from China, U.S. consumers are extremely wary, with one 2011 poll revealing that participants picked China 81 percent of the time when asked to choose two countries they perceived as having the least food safety oversight.[20] Chinese consumers are not much more confident about their domestic food supply. A 2011 survey found that food safety is a major concern for almost 70 percent of Chinese consumers[21] and there are regular reports of Chinese tourists emptying store shelves in other countries in search of infant formula not produced in China.

One tool that U.S. consumers do have is labeling. Thanks to federal labeling requirements, country of origin labeling is required for beef, pork, lamb, chicken, goat meat, wild and farm-raised fish and shellfish, perishable agricultural commodities (fruits and vegetables), peanuts, pecans, ginseng, and macadamia nuts. But these labeling rules do not apply to processed forms of these foods, and the USDA's definition of processing is far too broad, which excludes many foods from the labeling requirement. The U.S. rules for labeling meat have also been challenged at the World Trade Organization (WTO), resulting in a process of revising the rules that is ongoing.

U.S. Food Imports From China

After joining the World Trade Organization in 2001, China's food exports to the United States tripled to 4.1 billion pounds of food in 2012.[22] In addition to Chinese firms exporting to the United States, U.S. food and agribusiness companies have capitalized on China's cheap labor costs and weak regulations, hoping to sell to a growing class of Chinese consumers and export to the United States.

Total U.S. food imports from China fell during the economic recession, but over the past four years, imports have increased by about 250 million pounds, a 7 percent increase from 2009 to 2012.[23] Fruits and vegetables (primarily frozen and processed) make up most of the U.S. imports from China, amounting to 1.6 billion pounds and 41 percent of imported food products. 1.2 billion pounds of fresh, frozen and processed fish and seafood products made up about a third of imports (30 percent.)[24]

Most Chinese exports to the United States are fruits and vegetables that can be harvested and processed with lower labor costs in China than elsewhere,[25] undercutting U.S. farmers. As the world's largest apple producer, for example, China's apple juice concentrate exports supply a growing share of American's apple juice. By 2007, half the garlic Americans ate was grown in China, although that figure fell to 31 percent in 2011 as the recession and falling dollar dampened import demand.[26] Before China entered the WTO, the United States produced about 70 percent of the garlic Americans consumed.[27] Over the past decade, imports of Chinese garlic more than quadrupled, while U.S. garlic cultivation dropped by a third.[28]

The millions of pounds of imports from China represent a considerable portion of the food eaten by U.S. consumers. For example, in 2011:

- Eighty percent of the tilapia Americans ate came from the 382.2 million pounds of imports from China.

- The United States imported 367 million gallons of apple juice from China, amounting to almost half (49.6 percent) of U.S. consumption.
- The 70.7 million pounds of cod imported from China amounted to just more than half (51 percent) of U.S. consumption.
- The 217.5 million pounds of imported garlic was 31.3 percent of U.S. consumption.
- The 39.3 million pounds of frozen spinach represented 11 percent of U.S. consumption. (For more import quantities, see chart in Appendix I.)

Other Chinese exports include processed foods and food ingredients, products which most consumers purchase without considering where they came from. China is a leading supplier to the United States of ingredients like xylitol, used as a sweetener in candy, and sorbic acid, a preservative.[29] China supplies around 85 percent of U.S. imports of artificial vanilla, as well as many vitamins that are frequently added to food products, like folic acid and thiamine.[30] By 2007, 90 percent of America's vitamin C supplements came from China, and by 2010, China supplied the United States with 88 million pounds of candy.[31] The United States also imported 102 million pounds of sauces, including soy sauce; 81 million pounds of spices; 79 million pounds of dog and cat food; and 41 million pounds of pasta and baked goods from China in 2010.[32]

<u>U.S. Regulation of Chinese Food Imports</u>

U.S. oversight of Chinese food processors has not remotely kept pace with the growth in imports. Though the Food and Drug Administration prevented 9,000 unsafe Chinese products from entering the country between 2006 and 2010,[33] it is not because of vigilant inspection at U.S borders and ports. The agency's low inspection rate — less than 2 percent of imported produce, processed food and seafood[34] — almost guarantees that unsafe Chinese products are making their way into American grocery stores.

Other importers of food from China have instituted more intensive testing regimes for Chinese imports. From 2004 to 2009, Japan tested between 15 and 18 percent of food products from China, and up to 38 percent of frozen vegetables.[35]

In 2007, the FDA's director of the Center for Food Safety and Applied Nutrition stated that the growing Chinese food exports have "outstretched and outgrown the regulatory system for imports in the U.S."[36] During the melamine-tainted pet food crisis, it took the FDA one month to even identify their regulatory counterparts in China.[37]

In 2007, China consented to allow FDA inspectors to be stationed in China, and the FDA opened its first office in 2008.[38] However, the few FDA inspectors in China were overwhelmed by the sheer size of the nation's food production, including an estimated 1 million food-processing companies.[39] Between 2001 and 2008, the FDA inspected 46 food firms in China — less than six a year.[40] After the spate of import scandals, the FDA increased inspections, but still only conducted 13 food inspections in China from June 2009 to June 2010.[41] In fiscal year 2012, FDA conducted 10 inspections of food facilities in China.[42] Recently, the agency instituted a sampling program for *Salmonella* for pet food, pet treats and pet nutritional supplements, but only for domestic products.[43] The new testing program does not cover imports, despite the large volume and troubled safety record of pet food and treats imported from China.

Meat and poultry imports are the responsibility of the U.S. Department of Agriculture. Until 2009, FSIS conducted in-depth annual on-site audits of countries eligible to export meat, poultry and egg products to the United States. The department recently announced that in 2009 it made a major change to this system by ending annual visits to exporting countries, and instead starting to rely on a "Self-Reporting Tool" for countries as a substitute to annual audit visits. With this change, USDA began conducting audit visits every three years instead of annually and the agency stopped the practice of publishing the audit results of individual foreign meat, poultry, egg plants that exported products to the United States. This weakening of oversight of foreign meat and poultry producers does not yet impact products from China, because the country has not yet been approved to ship these products to the United States. But China is in the process of being certified "equivalent" to U.S. meat inspection standards and therefore eligible to export products.

Poultry

The USDA's actions with regard to China's interest in exporting poultry products to the United States offers a telling example of how the pressure to increase trade can leave food safety concerns as a lower priority. Currently, the United States does not permit poultry imports from China. U.S. agribusinesses have invested heavily in Chinese chicken production and processing – both to feed Chinese consumers and as a future export platform to U.S. consumers – and they have been working to get USDA approval for Chinese poultry exports to the United States.

In 2006, the USDA rapidly finalized China's request to begin exporting processed chicken to the United States the very same day as a visit from China's president.[44] This action apparently prompted China to resume negotiations over lifting its ban on American beef, instituted in 2003 after the discovery of mad cow disease in the state of Washington.[45]

Despite the Bush Administration's public blessing of Chinese chicken, the USDA's internal inspection reports of Chinese poultry facilities showed egregious food safety problems, including mishandling raw chicken throughout the processing areas, failing to perform *E. coli* and *Salmonella* testing, and routinely using dirty tools and equipment.[46] As these internal reports emerged, Congress refused to implement the Bush Administration proposal, effectively maintaining a ban on Chinese poultry imports.[47]

China contended the U.S. prohibition against chicken, produced in unsafe plants with insufficient inspection, was an illegal trade barrier. The World Trade Organization agreed in September 2010.[48] The same month, China announced it would impose high tariffs on American chicken products for allegedly being priced too cheaply.[49]

In January 2011, Chinese President Hu Jintao again visited the United States, cementing tens of billion of dollars in trade deals with the Obama Administration.[50] Shortly after this visit, the USDA announced new steps it had taken to honor China's request to export chicken to the United States.[51]

Currently, the USDA's Food Safety and Inspection Service is working through the steps to approve China as an exporter of poultry products to the United States, with the next step in the approval process expected to be completed in the fall. This process continues to proceed, even as the poultry sector in China is suffering mounting economic damage from a growing avian influenza outbreak.[52]

The processed poultry products being considered for approval are supposed to be made in Chinese plants from birds that have been sent from "approved" sources, including the United States or Canada, but not China. But without stationing USDA inspectors in Chinese processing plants, it will be virtually impossible to verify that these products are made from birds from approved sources rather than Chinese producers.

Organic and Third Party Certification

Organic products from China have not been immune from food safety concerns. Organic beans and berries imported from China have been rejected by the FDA for high pesticide levels, despite the fact that synthetic pesticides are not allowed under the USDA organic label.[53] More recently, testing conducted by U.S. media outlets found pesticide contamination of an organic ginger product sold in the United States.[54]

According to USDA's National Organic Program, from 1995 to 2006, the value of organic food exported from China rose from $300,000 to $350 million and vegetables, field crops and tea were China's largest organic exports.[55] In 2006, there were 496 operations in China certified as meeting U.S. organic standards and by 2010 that number had risen to 649 operations.[56]

In the United States, the USDA sets organic standards and third party certifiers are responsible for inspecting farms and food processors to ensure they are meeting the standards. In 2010, the USDA visited China to conduct an audit of four of the ten certifiers operating there. The agency reported that conditions "pose challenging oversight duties and responsibilities for certifying agents operating in China. Additionally, the size of China's land mass and higher financial margins in the organic industry could pose potential for fraud, especially by those outside of the organic certification system."[57]

In 2010, USDA banned one of the third party certifiers operating in China because the organization used Chinese government employees to inspect state-controlled farms.[58] But the challenge of operating truly independent third party auditing or inspection operations in China is not isolated to organic certification.

The FDA Food Safety Modernization Act, which became law in January 2011, instructs the FDA to establish a reliable system of audits conducted by foreign governments or other third parties for imported foods. A 2012 GAO report outlines the significant obstacles to doing this.[59] FDA has struggled in the past to oversee inspection activities conducted on contract to the agency by state governments,[60] a task that should be much simpler than coordinating with third parties and foreign governments around the world. To build the infrastructure and IT system necessary to oversee third party certifiers in countries such as China, where third parties and even government agencies must be accredited by another government agency,[61] seems like it will be an extraordinarily challenging project for the agency.

China's Food Safety System

Chinese officials have readily acknowledged the country's food system as "grim."[62] The country's decentralized and overlapping regulatory system has not been able to address China's sprawling food-processing industry. Repeated government efforts to reform food safety rules have so far failed to stem the tide of adulterated food. After a major food safety law from 2009 went into effect, a professor at the Chinese Academy of Governance stated that poor coordination between agencies, lackluster enforcement and inadequate government oversight hindered the enforcement of food safety laws.[63] It remains to be seen if an overhaul of the food safety system, announced in 2012, will manage to coordinate efforts government-wide and tighten food safety standards.[64]

The situation for Chinese consumers can be more dire than what U.S. and other export customers face. China usually exports the highest-quality food the country produces, leaving Chinese consumers vulnerable to the lower-quality products that remain.[65]

Reports on food safety problems since 2009 yield a long list of problems in both the domestic food supply and exported products. One persistent trend is "economically motivated adulteration," or what has been described as a culture of adulteration in China's agricultural sector.[66] Melamine contamination in Chinese food continues to be a problem, with a crackdown on melamine in milk powder in 2010 resulting in 96 arrests and 26 public officials being fired[67] and U.S. regulators finding high levels of melamine in a dog food shipment in January 2011.[68] After increased attention to the problem of melamine, some Chinese dairy producers appear to have switched to a new protein adulterant that is even more difficult to detect — hydrolyzed leather protein made from scraps of animal skin.[69]

Even veterinary drugs banned in China — such as clenbuterol, administered to animals to give them leaner meat and pinker skin — remain widely used in China despite years of documented consumer illnesses from residues in meat and organs,[70] and controversies over athletes avoiding meat for fear of testing positive for the performance enhancing drug.

Honey from China has continued to be a source of controversy. Illegal antibiotics are commonly found in Chinese honey imports. China dominates the international honey market and became the largest U.S. honey source after joining the WTO, supplying more than 70 million pounds by 2006.[71] For years, regulators had closely scrutinized Chinese honey for drug residues, including one that can be fatal.[72] In 2010, the FDA seized large amounts of Chinese honey after finding illegal antibiotics.[73]

Another trend is pesticide residues that remain on fruit, vegetables and processed foods when they enter the food supply. China is the world's largest pesticide producer and exporter.[74] In 2010, Chinese authorities found a banned, highly toxic pesticide in cowpeas, a legume similar to black-eyed peas.[75] China has largely failed to address illegal or dangerous chemical residues on food, evident in its weak maximum residue levels. The United States has established maximum residue levels (MRLs) for 77 pesticides used in garlic production and 112 pesticides used in apples orchards; of these, China has only 2 and 23 MRLs, respectively.[76]

Since 2009, the Chinese government has made a point of making public displays of enforcing food safety rules, inspecting food facilities and punishing people connected with tainted food. News reports frequently reference millions of inspections of facilities and frequent "crackdowns" on particular products. A search of news reports reveals a variety of enforcement efforts:

- The scandal over melamine-contaminated infant formula led to the execution of two people and prison terms for dairy company executives. [77]
- In 2011, industry and commerce authorities reported 62,000 cases of substandard food, leading to 43,000 unlicensed operations being shut down and 251 cases being sent to the judicial system. [78]
- A 2011 crackdown on food safety violations resulted in 2,000 arrests and 4,900 businesses being closed.[79]
- The Chinese news agency Xinhua reported in June 2012 that authorities shut down 5,700 unlicensed food businesses and discovered 15,000 cases of "substandard food" so far that year.[80]
- In early May 2013, news reports described a Chinese government campaign to break up a fake meat operation, leading to arrests of more than 900 people accused of passing off more than $1 million of rat meat as mutton.[81]

Ironically, the recent discovery of more than 7,000 dead pigs in the Huangpu River was actually described in some media reports as "an encouraging step forward in Chinese public health," because it indicated that rather than sell diseased animals into the food supply, producers dumped them into the river instead.[82]

But despite the concerted effort to show that the government is tough on food safety violators, problems persist. A small sample of recent food safety problems:

- In 2010, a scandal erupted over the use of food coloring and bleach to plump up shriveled old peas so they would appear fresh.[83]
- Authorities detected plasticizers, chemicals linked to immune and reproductive system damage, in samples of a leading brand of a common distilled white liquor.[84]
- Testing by Greenpeace of 18 varieties of tea found that every sample contained at least three different kinds of pesticides. 12 of the samples showed traces of banned pesticides.[85]

- In September 2012, FDA refused 10 shipments of canned mushrooms from China due to pesticide contamination, resulting in the Chinese government halting exports of canned mushrooms to the United States.[86]
- China Central Television reported in 2012 that testing of preserved fruit from 16 different companies found excessive pigments, bleaching agents and preservatives, as well as incorrect expiration dates.[87]
- The Xinhua News Agency reported in 2012 that wholesale vegetable dealers in Shandong province were found spraying cabbages with formaldehyde, presumably to preserve them during transport without refrigeration.[88]
- A 2012 report noted that fish vendors in Beijing were using a chemical used for temporary dental fillings to tranquilize fish during transport. [89]

Another recurring theme is lack of transparency. China's food safety enforcement system lacks the transparency necessary to warn the public about dangerous products or deter dangerous food-processing practices. The USDA reports that the Chinese government zealously guards the food safety data it collects, making it difficult to impartially evaluate China's food safety performance.[90] In 2010, some officials criticized regional authorities that publicized a widespread case of pesticide adulteration rather than obeying the "unspoken rule" of keeping food safety problems hidden from the public.[91] The father of one child sickened by melamine-tainted milk powder was jailed, and eventually paroled, for his activism on the issue.[92]

Lack of transparency is also evident in an ongoing problem with imported pet treats from China. Since 2007, thousands of American dogs have fallen ill or died after eating chicken jerky treats made in China. The FDA reports "from 2003, when China first approached the USDA about poultry exports, to 2011, the volume of pet food exports (regulated by the FDA) to the United States from China has grown 85-fold."[93] In August 2012, four months after visiting Chinese processing plants that export pet treats to the United States, the FDA published inspection reports that revealed that the factories refused to allow U.S. inspectors to collect samples for independent analysis.[94] Ultimately, testing done by the New York Department of Agriculture and Markets found contamination of some of the treats with residues of an undisclosed antibiotic, triggering voluntary recalls of the products by the manufacturer.[95]

U.S. Policies to Address Unsafe Food Imports

The WTO's Agreement on Agriculture has been a failure for farmers in the United States and has encouraged the growth of export platforms in places like China that benefit from low wages and weak regulatory standards, putting consumers around the world at risk. Congress and the Obama administration must revisit the current trade agenda to make public health, environmental standards and consumer safety the highest priorities when making decisions about trade policy. Specifically:

- The USDA should restart the process of determining if China's poultry inspection system is equivalent to the U.S. system and conduct an entirely new investigation before allowing Chinese poultry products to be exported to the United States.

- The USDA needs the resources to increase current levels of inspection of imported meat and poultry. If Chinese poultry products are approved for export to the United States, the USDA should permanently assign inspection personnel to China so that the exporting plants receive regular visits by USDA inspectors.

- The FDA needs the resources to effectively inspect the growing volume of food imports from China and other countries. Congress and the Obama Administration must instruct and provide adequate funding for the FDA to increase import inspections, and to increase the rigor of those inspections to include testing for pathogens and chemical, pesticide and drug residues, and to increase inspection of processed food ingredients.

- The FDA needs the resources to conduct inspections in food facilities in China, rather than relying on third-party certifications of the safety practices used by exporting firms. The use of third-party certifications in China has already been shown to be questionable in the certification used for organic products and in pilot projects on aquaculture conducted by the FDA. This type of system should not be used as a substitute for safety inspection by U.S. government inspectors.

- The USDA should close the loopholes in the current country of origin labeling rules and expand them to processed meats, fruits and vegetables. Congress should also require mandatory country of origin labeling for foods not currently covered by existing law, to require basic manufacturing information about where, and by what company, processed foods were produced.

APPENDIX 1

Food Product	U.S. Imports from China (Millions of Pounds)				Share of U.S. Consumption				
	2009	2010	2011	2012	2008	2009	2010	2011	4-Year Average
Tilapia	288.3	349.5	318.5	382.2	73.2%	77.8%	78.7%	80.2%	77.5%
Apple Juice (Mil. Gall.)	451.4	463.7	342.0	367.0	69.0%	70.0%	72.3%	49.6%	65.2%
Cod	63.2	71.4	78.9	70.7	59.4%	50.0%	50.4%	51.0%	52.7%
Mushrooms, Processing	78.1	78.6	68.2	68.4	53.7%	42.7%	22.4%	17.8%	34.1%
Garlic, All Uses	245.4	234.3	226.9	217.5	23.1%	22.8%	32.4%	31.3%	27.4%
Clams	17.0	19.8	24.1	27.4	9.0%	12.7%	19.0%	23.5%	16.1%
Spinach, Frozen	32.2	32.5	36.2	39.3	16.0%	21.5%	15.3%	11.0%	16.0%
Crab	18.9	23.7	22.9	22.9	15.0%	10.4%	13.5%	14.3%	13.3%
Salmon	71.4	88.1	86.4	72.7	10.8%	11.1%	14.4%	14.3%	12.7%
Peaches, Canned	91.8	109.8	92.0	98.5	11.8%	9.1%	9.0%	8.1%	9.5%
Cauliflower, Processing	11.1	8.9	1.3	8.1	12.0%	14.6%	7.8%	0.9%	8.8%
Shrimp	97.1	106.0	94.7	78.6	8.6%	7.8%	8.7%	7.3%	8.1%
Pineapples, Canned	65.2	52.7	40.6	26.2	9.7%	8.7%	7.1%	5.8%	7.8%
Pears, Canned	53.0	57.2	49.4	50.7	7.3%	7.0%	7.6%	8.1%	7.5%
Asparagus, Frozen	1.4	1.1	0.8	0.2	10.7%	12.2%	3.4%	1.9%	7.1%
Catfish/Pangasius	22.8	17.9	10.8	7.9	2.7%	1.6%	14.4%	5.6%	6.1%
Broccoli, Processed	29.4	25.7	30.4	25.9	3.7%	4.9%	3.4%	3.7%	3.9%
Green Peas, Frozen	16.6	20.4	10.3	5.7	4.2%	3.5%	4.2%	2.3%	3.5%
Cherries, Sweet, Canned	0.1	0.6	0.0	0.3	0.0%	1.9%	8.4%		3.4%
Onions, Dried	5.5	4.3	2.8	3.1	5.9%	5.1%	0.9%	0.6%	3.1%
Apples, Canned	32.4	18.7	17.4	31.9	2.5%	3.0%	1.8%	1.8%	2.3%
Canned Tuna	18.6	17.6	40.7	52.5	0.0%	1.9%	2.1%	5.1%	2.3%
Pears, Fresh	24.3	11.6	13.8	12.4	2.8%	2.5%	1.2%	1.5%	2.0%
Strawberries, Frozen	7.1	10.8	9.1	5.7	1.2%	1.3%	0.0%	0.0%	0.6%
Mushroom, Fresh	10.6	10.6	11.4	13.0	1.3%	1.4%	1.4%	1.4%	1.4%
Artichoke, All Uses	3.5	2.1	2.4	1.4	1.6%	1.9%	0.5%	0.5%	1.1%

Sources: USDA FAS GATS database; USDA Economic Research Service. Vegetable and Melon Yearbook 2011 and Fruit and Tree Nut Outlook 2012; U.S. National Fisheries Institute. "Top 10 Consumed Seafoods." 2012.

APPENDIX 2

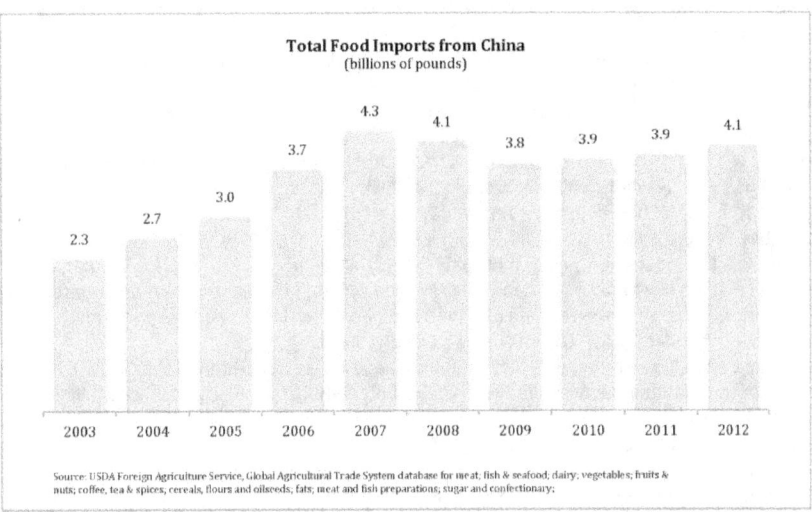

Total food imports from China fell during the economic recession, but over the past four years, imports have increased by about 250 million pounds, a 7 percent increase from 2009 to 2012.

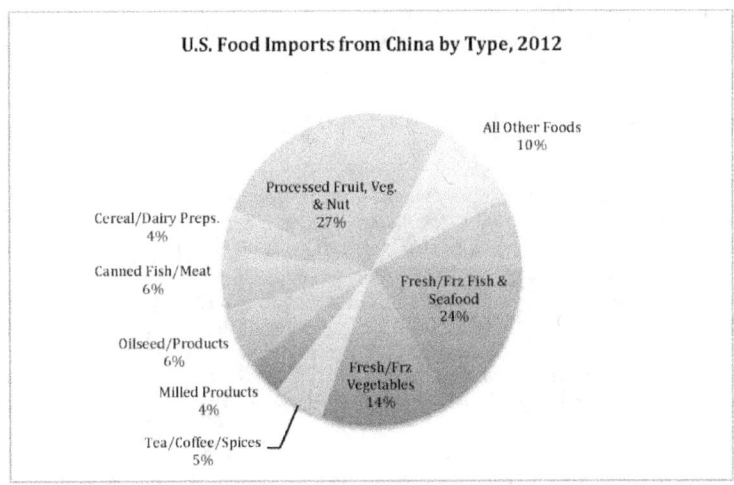

Source: USDA FAS GATS.

Fruits and vegetables (primarily frozen and processed) made up the plurality of imports from China, amounting to 1.6 billion pounds and 41 percent of the imported food products. The 1.2 billion in fresh, frozen and processed fish and seafood products made up about a third of the imports (30 percent).

[1] U.S. Government Accountability Office. "Food Safety: FDA Can Better Oversee Food Imports by Assessing and Leveraging Other Countries' Oversight Resources." GAO-12-933. September 2012 at 1 and 5.

[2] U.S. Department of Agriculture Economic Research Service (USDA ERS). Table 1 – Import Shares of US food consumption using the volume method. May 30, 2012. Available at http://www.ers.usda.gov/topics/international-markets-trade/us-agricultural-trade/import-share-of-consumption.aspx#import. Accessed April 22, 2013.

[3] Lohmar, Bryan et al. USDA ERS. "China's Ongoing Agricultural Modernization." EIB-51. April 2009 at 1.

[4] United Nations Food and Agriculture Organization (UN FAO). FAOStat. Country rank in the world, by commodity (quantity): China. Based on most recent data available, 2008. Available at http://faostat.fao.org/. Accessed December 14, 2010.

[5] Barboza, David. "U.S. Court Fines Chinese Vitamin C Makers." *New York Times*. March 15, 2013.

[6] "Mix of chemicals may be key to pet-food deaths." *CNN*. May 1, 2007; U.S. Government Accountability Office. "Food and Drug Administration Overseas Offices have Taken Steps to Help Ensure Import Safety, but More Long-Term Planning is Needed." GAO-10-960. September 2010 at 1.

[7] Barboza, David and Alexei Barrionuevo. "Filler in Animal Feed is Open Secret in China." *New York Times*. April 30, 2007; Barboza, David. "Discovery of Melamine-Tainted Milk Shuts Shanghai Dairy." *New York Times*. January 2, 2010.

[8] "Mix of chemicals may be key to pet-food deaths." *CNN*. May 1, 2007.

[9] Barboza, David. "An Export Boom Suddenly Facing a Quality Crisis." *New York Times*. May 18, 2007; USDA. Press release. "Joint Update: FDA/USDA Update on Tainted Animal Feed." Release No. 0121.07. March 2, 2007.

[10] Gale, Fred and Jean Buzby. USDA ERS. "Imports from China and food safety issues." Economic Information Bulletin No. 52. July 2009 at 10.

[11] U.S. Department of Agriculture Foreign Agricultural Service (USDA FAS). Global Agricultural Trade System (HS-10: 230100090, 2309100010.)

[12] Food and Drug Administration. Public Health Focus: Melamine Contamination in China. January 5, 2009. Available at http://www.fda.gov/NewsEvents/PublicHealthFocus/ucm179005.htm.

[13] Ee Lyn, Tan. "China eyes milk test after melamine deaths scandal." *Reuters*. June 15, 2010; Peterkin, Tom. "China milk scandal: 53,000 children fall ill from contaminated milk powder." *The (London) Telegraph*. September 22, 2008.

[14] Ee Lyn. June 15, 2010.

[15] Spears, Lee and Helen Yuan. "China withdraws milk as Fonterra decries Sanlu delay." *Bloomberg News*. September 24, 2008.

[16] Spencer, Richard. "China tainted milk scandal: Heinz and Mars drawn in." *The (London) Telegraph*. September 30, 2008; "Melamine found in Cadbury goods." *BBC*. September 29, 2008; "Melamine found in more Chinese-made food products." *New York Times*. September 26, 2008; Koo, Heejin. "South Korea orders Mars, Nestle to recall products." *Bloomberg News*. October 4, 2008; YUM! Brands. U.S. Securities and Exchange Commission. SEC filings 10-k. 2007 at 3.Spencer. *The (London) Telegraph*.

[17] US Honey Makers Take a Swat at Chinese Smugglers. Andrew Schneider. AOL News. May 6 2010.

[18] Murphy, Joan. "Anti-dumping probe links large China shrimp exporter to transshipment." *Food Chemical News*. September 28, 2012.

[19] Food Sentry. Preliminary Analysis of International Food Safety Violations. Available at http://www.foodsentry.org/preliminary-analysis-of-international-food-safety-violations/. Accessed April 22, 2013.

[20] Baertlein, Lisa. "U.S. Shoppers Wary About China Food Safety: Survey" *Reuters*. January 19, 2011.

[21] "Nearly 70% of Chinese Consumers Do Not Trust Food Safety." *Arirang News*. January 3, 2011.

[22] USDA FAS. Global Agricultural Trade System. Available at www.fas.usda.gov/gats/. (Food includes consumption imports of meat; fish & seafood; dairy; vegetables, fruits & nuts, coffee, tea & spices; cereals, oil seeds; fats; meat & fish preparations; sugar & confectionery; cocoa; cereal & dairy preparations; vegetable & fruit preparations; and miscellaneous edible preparations contained in two-digit harmonized codes: HS-2: 02, 03, 04, 07, 08, 09, 10, 11, 12, 15, 16, 17, 18, 19, 20, 21, 22.)

[23] USDA FAS. Global Agricultural Trade System database for meat; fish & seafood; dairy; vegetables; fruits & nuts; coffee, tea & spices; cereals, flours and oilseeds; fats; meat and fish preparations; sugar and confectionary.

[24] USDA FAS. Global Agricultural Trade System.

[25] Gale, Fred et al. USDA Economic Research Service (ERS). "Investment in Processing Industry Turns Chinese Apples Into Juice Exports." FTS-344-01. October 2010 at 3.

[26] Gale and Buzby. USDA ERS. (2009) at iii; USDA FAS. Global Agricultural Trade System. USDA FAS GATS database; USDA ERS. Vegetable and Melon Yearbook 2011 and Fruit and Tree Nut Outlook 2012.

[27] USDA ERS. Fruit and Tree Nut Outlook Yearbook. 2010 at Table 16.

[28] USDA FAS. Global Agricultural Trade System. (Garlic, HS-10: 0703200020, 0703200010, 0712904040, 0712904020); USDA ERS. Vegetables and Melons Yearbook Data. 2009 (Updated May 20, 2010) at Table 5.

[29] Lee, Don. "China's additives on menu in U.S." *Los Angeles Times*. May 18, 2007.

[30] USDA FAS. Global Agricultural Trade System. (HS-10: 2912410000); Lee (2007).

[31] USDA FAS. Global Agricultural Trade System. (HS-6, 170490); Johnson, Tim. "China corners vitamin market." *Seattle Times*. June 3, 2007.

[32] USDA FAS. (HS-4, 1902 and 1905; HS-4, 2103; HS-10, 2309100090, 2039100010.)

[33] FDA. Import Refusal Database. Available at www.accessdata.fda.gov/scripts/importrefusals/. Accessed January-February 2011.

[34] FDA. Combined Field Activities – ORA. Program Activity Data. Field Foods Program Activity Data.

[35] Matsuda, Akane. "Food Safety Issues in the Vegetable Trade Between China and Japan: What Is Required to Establish Effective Food Safety Systems in the Bilateral Food Trade?" MPP Essay. Oregon State University, June 14, 2010.

[36] MacLeod, Calum. "China details new food-quality measures." *USA Today*. September 13, 2007.

[37] GAO (2010) at 12.

[38] Weisman, Steven. "China agrees to post U.S. safety officials in its food factories." *New York Times*. December 12, 2007; Zhe, Zhu. "U.S. food, drug agency opens Beijing office." *China Daily*. November 20, 2008.

[39] Lohmar, Bryan et al. USDA ERS. "China's Ongoing Agricultural Modernization." EIB-51. April 2009 at 24.

[40] Shames, Lisa. "Food Safety: FDA Could Strengthen Oversight of Imported Food by Improving Enforcement and Seeking Additional Authorities." GAO-10-699T. Testimony before the Subcommittee on Oversight and Investigations, U.S. House of Representatives Committee on Energy and Commerce. May 20, 2010 at 5.

[41] GAO. (2010) at 17.

[42] FDA. Combined Field Activities – ORA. Program Activity Data. Field Foods Program Activity Data.

[43] Food and Drug Administration. "CVM Issues Assignment to Collect and Analyze Samples of Pet Foods, Pet Treats, and Pet Nutritional Supplements in Interstate Commerce in the United States for *Salmonella*." March 22, 2013.

[44] Quaid, Libby. "U.S. to allow processed poultry shipments from China." *Associated Press*. April 20, 2006; 71 Fed. Reg. 20867–20871.

[45] Quaid. April 20, 2006; "U.S. tries to sell beef to China amid food disputes." *Reuters*. June 29, 2007.

[46] USDA Food Safety and Inspection Service. "Final report of an initial equivalence audit carried out in China covering China's poultry inspection system." May 17 2005 at 9-11.

[47] Pub. L. 110-161. Title VII. §733.

[48] World Trade Organization. "United States—Certain Measures Affecting Imports of Poultry from China: Report of the Panel." WT/DS392/R. September 29, 2010 at 183-184.

[49] "China to levy anti-dumping duty on U.S. Poultry." *Bloomberg News*. September 26. 2010.

[50] Oliphant, James. "Obama and Hu Jintao pledge cooperation, downplay differences." *Los Angeles Times*. January 19, 2011

[51] Bottemiller, Helena. "USDA Petitioned to Block Chinese Poultry." *Food Safety News*. January 31, 2011.

[52] UPI. "China avian flu hits poultry sector, losses mount." April 16, 2013.

[53] Gale and Buzby (2009) at 17.

[54] Clapp, Stephen. "USDA bans organic certification agency from operating in China." *Food Chemical News*. June 21, 2010.

[55] U.S. Department of Agriculture National Organic Program (USDA NOP). "2010 Organic Assessment of China." July 2011 at 3.

[56] USDA NOP (2011) at 4.

[57] USDA NOP (2011) at 9.

[58] Clapp, Stephen. (2010).

[59] GAO (2012).

[60] GAO (2012) at 25.

[61] GAO (2012) at 19.

[62] "Food safety situation still grim in China." *Associated Press*. March 3, 2009.

[63] "Chinese lawmakers call for enhancing supervision of food safety." *Xinhua*. February 25, 2010.

[64] "China Releases Five Year Food Safety Plan." *Food Safety News*. June 18, 2012.

[65] Bodeen, Christopher. "Here we go again: China denies food safety issues." *Associated Press*. May 23, 2007.

[66] Barboza and Barrionuevo (2007).

[67] "96 arrested in China for selling adulterated milk powder." IANS. January 13 2011.

[68] FDA. Import Refusal Report Database. Refusal Actions by FDA as Recorded in OASIS for China. January 2011. Accessed March 2, 2011 with code 72BCT99.

[69] Olesen, Alexa. "China warns dairy producers inspectors watching for toxic melamine and leather protein in milk." *Associated Press*. February 17, 2011.

[70] Olesen, Alexa. "Skinny pigs, poison pork: China battles farm drugs." *Associated Press*. January 24, 2011.

[71] USDA FAS. (HS-10: 04090000); FAO STAT. Country rank in the world, by commodity (quantity): China. Based on most recent data available, 2008. Accessed December 14, 2010.

[72] Schneider, Andrew. "Country of Origin no Guarantee on Cheap Imports." *Seattle Post-Intelligencer*. June 5, 2009.

[73] Fulton, April. "FDA seizes tainted Chinese honey after Sen. Schumer raises fuss." *National Public Radio*. June 11, 2010.

[74] Zhang, WenJun, FuBin Jiang, and JiangFeng Ou. "Global pesticide consumption and pollution: with China as a focus." Proceedings of the International Academy of Ecology and Environmental Sciences. 2011. 1(2): 125-144.

[75] Wong, Edward. "Officials in China at odds over food scandal." *New York Times*. March 2, 2010.

[76] USDA FAS. International Maximum Residue Levels Database. Available at www.mrldatabase.com/. Accessed March 2011.

[77] "China vows harsh penalties for food safety crimes." Associated Press. September 16, 2010.

[78] "62,000 illegal food cases in 11 months of 2011." Xinhua. January 10, 2012.

[79] Ramzy, Austin. "China Food Safety: Big Crackdown, but Big Concerns Remain." *Time*. August 5, 2011.

[80] McDonald, Mark. "From Milk to Peas, A Chinese Food-Safety Mess." *International Herald Tribune*. June 21, 2012.

[81] Martina, Michael and Sally Huang. "Chinese police bust million-dollar rat-meat ring." *Reuters*. May 3, 2013.

[82] Barboza, David. "A Tide of Death, but This Time Food Supply Is Safe." *New York Times*. March 14, 2013.

[83] Yan, Wang. "Fake green peas latest food scandal." *China Daily,* China. March 31, 2010.

[84] "China media: Chinese liquor scandal." *BBC News*. November 22, 2012.

[85] Greenpeace. "Pesticides: Hidden Ingredients in Chinese Tea." 2012 at 1-2.

[86] Booth, Amy. "Residue concerns keep Chinese canned mushrooms off U.S. market." *Food Chemical News*. November 23, 2012.

[87] "Preserved fruit in China Tainted." *The New Paper*. April 30, 2012.

[88] "Chinese sellers accused of spraying cabbage with formaldehyde." Associated Press. May 7, 2012.

[89] Zuo, Mandy. "Dental cement used to calm fish" *South China Morning Post*. March 22, 2012.

[90] Gale and Buzby (2009) at 4.

[91] Wong. March 2, 2010.

[92] MacLeod, Calum. "China's organic farms rooted in food safety concerns." *USDA Today*. January 24, 2011.

[93] FDA. "FDA Investigates Animal Illnesses Linked to Jerky Pet Treats." September 14, 2012. http://www.fda.gov/AnimalVeterinary/SafetyHealth/ProductSafetyInformation/ucm319463.htm

[94] Aleccia, JoNel. "China stiff-arms FDA on jerky pet treat testing, reports show." NBCnews.com. August 22, 2012.

[95] FDA. Recall—Firm Press Release. "Milo's Kitchen® Voluntarily Recalls Chicken Jerky and Chicken Grillers Home-style Dog Treats." January 9, 2013.

Mr. ROHRABACHER. Thank you very much. Ms. Richardson.

STATEMENT OF MS. SOPHIE RICHARDSON, CHINA DIRECTOR, HUMAN RIGHTS WATCH

Ms. RICHARDSON. Thank you, Mr. Chairman. And thanks to the members of the subcommittee for holding this timely——

Mr. ROHRABACHER. We are going to need you a little closer to the mic or whatever we can do there.

Ms. RICHARDSON. How is that?

Mr. ROHRABACHER. That is great.

Ms. RICHARDSON. In Human Rights Watch's view, the integrity of products made in China, whether they are for domestic consumption or for export is directly related to the government's respect for the freedom of expression, access to information, and the independence of the legal system. In other words, the lack of protections, the lack of upholding these particular rights make it extremely difficult to ensure whether products are safe, whether products are what they say they are, or whether consumers here or there have any means of real effective redress.

In one particularly telling example of the Chinese Government's choice to suppress information as Mr. Keating referred to in his opening remarks, Chinese journalists were ready in the early summer of 2008 to report the melamine scandal but because of the ban on bad news in the run up to the 2008 Olympics, those journalists were not allowed to report that story until much later in the year by which point 300,000 kids had gotten sick and at least 6 had died. So the government was perfectly willing to suppress news even that which posed a clear public safety threat.

It is also worth noting that in November 2010 a Beijing court sentenced a man named Zhao Lianhai to 2½ years in prison on charges of causing a public disturbance which we found particularly ironic description of the actions of man who in the face of his own child's melamine-induced illness had sought to organize other parents to file a class action lawsuit. Even now 5 years later, it is not hard to find newspaper articles about Chinese consumers either going abroad specifically for the purpose of or incidental to outside travel purchasing baby milk formula because concerns about those products still run so deep.

To us, it is of equal concern the range of issues on which the Chinese domestic press and the international press continue to be prevented from reporting in a timely manner, whether it is about chemical spills, infectious disease outbreaks or public unrest in response to environmental problems. This puts all of us at risk.

I think the problems aren't just a question of what does or doesn't make it into a newspaper or what products make it into an export stream, but also about what kinds of information ordinary people inside China can have access to. I have also submitted into the record a report we wrote in 2011 about the lead poisoning of children in four provinces in China. These were children of people who either worked in battery factories or lived near facilities that processed products made with lead. None of those facilities operated in compliance with domestic laws on health and safety obligations. Many of them were operating in violation of close-down orders. Several of them had been fined, but paid the fines and continued to operate. And we think this was largely a result of commingling of economic and political interests in those areas. It is a common dynamic across the country.

Parents of sick children were repeatedly thwarted, not only in their efforts to get accurate tests. Parents told us repeatedly about being given falsified test results. Parents who went to the provincial capital to file complaints or try to file lawsuits were turned back. Some of them, in fact, were arrested, essentially in pursuit of simply trying to get accurate diagnoses and some sort of compensation or assistance for their gravely-ill children.

I think it is the case that while there are more regulations than rhetoric now particularly coming out of the new leadership about pollution and about public health, it is very hard to see how those have become actionable tools for people to get educated, get help, or hold officials or companies to account.

On the question of what remains to be done, clearly, and many people at this table are much better equipped to talk about the regulatory regimes and what fixes there need to be taken than I am, but this is obviously I think consistent with, for example, ICE's problems and even accessing the facilities to check for prison-made goods. There is a long history of the challenges of inspections inside the country.

But I think it is also not just a question of regulation of inspection regimes. There are issues about information, freedom of express, at stake. And I think it is not just up to the State Department or specific cabinet members to raise those issues. I think it is very clear that for the FDA, for their agencies to talk about access to information and freedom of expression in China is more meaningful than it ever has been in the past.

I also think there is a lot of room for U.S. officials from a variety of agencies to take these issues up with counterparts other than the Foreign Ministry or the Ministry of Health, such as the Supreme Court or the Public Security Bureau. Thank you very much.

[Ms. Richardson did not submit a prepared statement.]

Mr. ROHRABACHER. Thank you very much. Thank all of you for beginning this discussion. It is the chair's intention to let Mr. Keating, the ranking member, go first in the questions and then Mr. Stockman from Texas, and then I will—I think they call it in baseball, I will clean up.

Mr. KEATING. Thank you, Mr. Chairman. I just had a thought listening to you, Ms. Richardson, that in the absence of the media being able to disclose things, what effect, if any, has the social media been able to do to get the word out to Chinese people that there are dangers in their food and specifically when these instances occur, and there is illness attached, to alert people in that respect? Has it been helpful in that way?

Ms. RICHARDSON. Certainly it is an incredibly powerful tool for alerting people to specifically which kinds of products or which companies' products are problematic. At the same time, first of all, social media is subject to the same kinds of censorship the official print media is or electronic media. And so sometimes that information is quashed fairly quickly.

I don't have a lot of specific research to point to this, but it is also become more common in the last 4 or 5 years for journalists and even sort of citizen journalists to be charged with spreading rumors. There is actually a specified—it is considered an administrative violation rather than a criminal one, but I think it makes some people nervous about sharing information that could be construed as reporting a rumor rather than a fact.

Mr. KEATING. Mr. Triplett, you mentioned the effects of this on America's business community here at home. Could you comment, and any of our panelists, on how it affects America's interests from a business perspective abroad with us trying to do business abroad?

Mr. TRIPLETT. Yes, sir. Of course, we know that the Chinese are the biggest counterfeiters in the world. And so it is one thing to counterfeit something and make it work right and so forth and so on, but if you make something that is, in fact, poisonous, then obviously you damage the brand of the American firm as well. I think that is a whole wider issue that you can get into. That gets into things besides consumables as well. There have been rumors for years about the Chinese having UL labels that were faked. And so somebody thinks abroad, let us say you see something that is made in the United States, has a UL label on it and if it is possibly faked by the Chinese, then obviously you lose business all the way around.

It is part of the whole larger thing which is one of the reasons why I am suggesting that the committee return to the idea of a comprehensive approach to the various kinds of Chinese problems. You all had hearings on Chinese cyber terrorism, correct? So that is an issue. Food safety is an issue. Arms smuggling, I would argue, is an issue, and so forth and so on. And to the extent that the Congress can look at this comprehensively, I think that is probably a good idea. Thank you.

Mr. KEATING. To any of our panelists, Chinese officials have been making some attempts to increase regulation and enforcement targeting polluting factories. Have these attempts been making a difference at all in addressing the urgent and long-term health consequences associated with the levels of lead seen in villages like Henan, and Hunan, Shaanxi, and Yunnan. Those kind of villages, there are reports that there is lead polluting those villages. Are any of you aware of the efforts they are making on trying to regulate this kind of pollution, if they are effective at all?

Ms. LOVERA. I am not familiar specifically with lead programs, but I mean when we look at food safety stories and we are trying to track what is coming out of China, it does appear that there is kind of a broad attempt to really put on a very public effort to crack down on problems. There is something often in the news about the crackdown. Last week it was fake meat. It is pretty constant. I mean one of the issues when you are talking about something that is as pervasive as entire villages being contaminated, the question is then where are you going to grow the food? The lead is not just going to go away because they deal with the polluting factor. It is in the soil.

Why I can speak to the best is that we don't have a regulatory system here to know what province or let alone village a product would come from if it was shipped here and we don't really have a system that is going to very often do a lab test to look for lead levels. We tend to find that kind of thing when there is a problem and work backwards and then find a source. We are not intercepting things when they are coming into the U.S.

Mr. KEATING. I have a question. Go ahead.

Ms. RICHARDSON. I would just add to that a couple of points. Shortly after we released this report about lead poisoning, there was an announcement by the Ministry of Environment that about 500 battery-producing factories were going to be shut down. We have tried to track that over the years to see if they actually were shut down, if they stayed shut down, if, in fact, they reopened, whether the necessary protective practices had been put in place and it is extremely difficult to discern whether that has actually happened.

Look, we see this on lots of different issues of a problem reaches a certain level of publicity inside China. The government says we are going to crack down on it. And a year later we are having the same conversation. I did also want to pick up on the point that Ms. Lovera just made because when we were doing this research, we were also trying to figure out if any of the batteries that were being produced in these factories actually were turning up in the U.S. or were being on sold into an export chain. It was either going from the China end to here or going from here backwards. It was almost impossible to figure out. We didn't have the resources to try to track the products along the way. So for all I know, products that got made in these very factories wound up here. But we should be able to know that. We should be able to figure that out more easily I think.

Mr. KEATING. Thank you. And I yield back, Mr. Chairman.

Mr. ROHRABACHER. Thank you and now Mr. Stockman.

Mr. STOCKMAN. I have a question. If we—first of all, I would have expected Diane Sawyer or someone from ABC, NBC, CBS, anybody to cover this. This is a national problem. My question for you is, if we publicize your names and make some statements, some of the frustrations I get when I am on a committee I will reiterate some of the things and I am not saying you have done this, then the press calls up and they say well, that is not exactly what we said.

I think this is very alarming what we are hearing today and had another nation or other nations done this, I think many people would view it almost as an act of war. And that is alarming. Ms. Richardson, your statement that they allowed their own citizens to die just so they could have a good face on the Olympics and that they are willing to sacrifice their own children, their own children for the purpose of national pride. I don't think then that we fall anywhere near their own children. So I don't see how their concerns, what I am saying is if they don't seem to care about their own kids, why would they care about us? They can't run their own food program, but they are somehow going to have compassion for us? That is simply not true.

I was wondering, which company, is Walmart one of the ones that imports the most Chinese food for their groceries, do you know?

Mr. KASTEL. It is really across the board. The organic industry has been the subject of corporate takeover so to speak through mergers and acquisitions, so most of the major name brands are controlled by familiar agribusinesses like Dean Foods and General Mills and Kraft and Smuckers.

Mr. STOCKMAN. Have you gone to those farms that claim to be organic in China?

Mr. KASTEL. No.

Mr. STOCKMAN. Would they let you come there?

Mr. KASTEL. No. This is a really good question. I mean they will limit our access. As an industry watchdog, we actually had some inspectors on the ground before the melamine problem reared its ugly head. These people withdrew. In fact, we had two sets of independent, nonprofit inspectors. They weren't necessarily experts in terms of agriculture. They were normally inspecting workplace environments, but both groups of inspectors withdrew because they were afraid for their own personal safety. They couldn't get near these facilities.

It is even worse. Now you are a consumer of organic food?

Mr. STOCKMAN. Yes.

Mr. KASTEL. We appreciate that. The farmers that are members of the Cornucopia Institute and the farmers that are certified under the USDA accreditation program are visited every year by a USDA accredited certifier. The USDA directly supervises these certifiers, so there is this third party oversight and then you have got nonprofit, public interest groups watching the corporations and watching the government officials. That doesn't happen in China. There are no U.S. certification agencies. All the USDA certification happens by foreign certifiers mostly from Europe. They can't even go unencumbered and inspect these farms. They have to be accompanied by a Chinese certification entity. The farmland is actually owned by the state, not by the individual farmers. It is a whole different animal over there.

The individual farms are not even being certified as our farms here are as a separate farming operation where their procedures are very intimately reviewed and scrutinized. Instead, because of the cumbersome mechanism, it is so expensive to certify farms over there, like a couple thousand dollars that most of these very small agricultural producers are certified under a group or an umbrella certification through the exporters. So it is a bastardization of the entire system that organic consumers in this country are willing to pay a premium for.

I think you used the term Orwellian? Was that you, Representative?

Mr. STOCKMAN. Yes.

Mr. KASTEL. This is Orwellian that families are seeking a safer and more nutritious food supply that they trust and it is coming from this low level of oversight. And you asked about the competition that we face. Our farmers, our entrepreneurs, our processors, our high-integrity businesses are facing this unfair, uneven playing field because we go through—we jump through these hoops. It is expensive. We have to document everything we are doing on farms and processing plants. That is not happening in China.

Mr. STOCKMAN. I want to say one thing. I actually toured a catfish farm in China and I had the PLA there very close to me. It was owned by—people don't realize it, but the military actually owns a lot of the industries over there. And it was alarming to me to the degree which they controlled it and we were given limited access. I can just say though I am puzzled, why do you think you are not—well two questions, excuse me, Mr. Chairman, if I go over a little bit. But should we block all imports of food until we get access? And two, why do you think that the national media is not picking up on this? It is alarming that they are not.

Mr. KASTEL. Sure. First of all, I think as a food consumer, as I think we all are, I would like to see Congress demand of our regulators that imported foods meet the same high standards, the same level of inspections. Just because it is coming in on a container, why should there be less oversight? If we can afford to do it, they can afford to do it in other countries, either through a creditable inspection service with which we recognize reciprocity which doesn't exist in China or by our own inspectors. But short of that, do you want to entrust your children, your grandchildren's health and future and well being to some economic interest?

Again, this has been referenced more than just by my testimony. We have endemic levels of commercial fraud in that country, superseding just the food industry. Why should we trust somebody who has robbed us 20 times that they are going to operate in an ethical manner going forward? Trust and verify.

Mr. STOCKMAN. Thank you.

Ms. LOVERA. Just on the topic, I mean one issue that we deal with as a consumer advocacy group is a little bit of almost fatigue on food safety news and I think that is part of what is happening. But to your question about whether to let these products in or not, we are now very dependent on certain things. One country, like China, is producing 80 percent of the world's Vitamin C and you shut them down, products won't get made, right? So that is one factor in this as a reluctance to not have some of the products made.

I mean one very specific example we are dealing with right now is the FDA has been tracking for several years reports of illness in mostly dogs, and it seems to be tied to a specific type of treats made of chicken. They are like chicken jerky treats. And they are sourced from China. They can't quite figure out the problem and this has been going on for years. It will get occasional local media, people will cover it as a local story, this tragic thing happened to a local pet owner, but it hasn't really risen to this thing that has been going on for several years. There is a China connection and at several points last year when FDA went to plants that were making some of these ingredients, they were not allowed to take samples. They could take samples, but they couldn't send the samples to labs in the U.S. to do the testing, so it was a real breakdown in our regulators' ability to figure out what is going on.

So that gets covered almost as a local story, a very personal story, but there is a much bigger story there about our system not being able to deal with this and we are dependent on the companies doing a voluntary recall. We haven't seen FDA block this product.

Mr. STOCKMAN. Yes, I remember when the national media got upset with the dog food thing. I was surprised that all the dog food was made in China at one place, even though you paid $10 for this bag, $2 for this bag came from the same shop.

Mr. Chairman, I yield back the balance of my overtime use.

Mr. ROHRABACHER. If we have more time and if you want more time for a second round, we can. We are expecting to have a vote very shortly.

Let me just ask you some, as I say clean up, batting clean up here. You mentioned Vitamin C, 80 percent of the world's Vitamin C comes from China?

Ms. LOVERA. Yes.

Mr. ROHRABACHER. Is there any question that some Vitamin C may not be up to standard?

Ms. LOVERA. That is an assumption on our part. I can't prove that to you, but I am assuming that there is some problems based on the track record we have seen in other sectors.

Mr. ROHRABACHER. Do we know if—here it is, my multi-vitamin for every time I have a meal and the Vitamin C is in there. Do I know where that Vitamin C is coming from?

Ms. LOVERA. No, we don't get this level of information as consumers.

Mr. ROHRABACHER. So American consumer, if some of us are concerned with the standards in China, we don't know that we are consuming something from China even—and that's not on anywhere near on the label, right?

Ms. LOVERA. It may tell you what country it is made in as a processed food, but it's not going to go down every ingredient.

Mr. KASTEL. Can I add, Mr. Chairman?

Mr. ROHRABACHER. Go right ahead.

Mr. KASTEL. Besides for those supplements that you are shaking, that Vitamin C ascorbic acid is a very, very common food ingredient in processed food, so if you read the fine print where those little novels are on the side of a food package, that is in there. So there was some——

Mr. ROHRABACHER. And it doesn't say where it is coming from?

Mr. KASTEL. No, it doesn't.

Mr. ROHRABACHER. It just says Vitamin C is in there, fine, but I personally go out of my way to try to not buy products in China because I have concluded, that is one of the reasons we are holding this hearing is because the chairman has concluded that there are some major questions that need to be answered and some challenges that need to be met before we can trust our putting things into our body or into our family's body that might be harmful.

Mr. KASTEL. Industry has fought like hell against country of origin labeling, COO. We would really encourage this body and all Members of Congress to defend the rights of the American public to make informed choices in the marketplace. Not only do I not want to buy Chinese food in my household, I want to reward the businesses in the United States that employ people at fair wages, that meet pollution and other regulatory standards, that meet other labor standards. And I can't do that in most of the food I buy because the processed food, as Patty was stating, is not required to label.

Mr. ROHRABACHER. I actually shop a lot for my family. I like to shop. And I know I am going to shock everybody here, but I really like to go to the 99 cent store, okay? So I go to the 99 cent store and you have all of these labels that are sounding so American, I mean Honey Hill and Aunt Martha's this and all of these things that sound just sound so down home American and then you look real close and the little tiny print it says China on it.

Mr. KASTEL. It is even worse than that, you have brands like Chicago Pneumatic that makes tools. They are from China. Maybe there is a town called Chicago in one of the provinces there, but I don't think so.

Mr. ROHRABACHER. Or as the one that used to be, they changed the name of a city in China to USA so they can print on it made in USA. Hm. Well, we are up against what I consider to be a very, how do we say, an adversary that is seeking benefit in a way that will put our children and our families at risk and we need to make sure that—and there are people in our country, of course, who are making a profit by dealing with those who are putting us at risk. And I think that we need to make sure that number one, labeling means something.

I will give you one example. In my area, there is a gentleman who runs a paint and coating company and he used to sell all the paint for Mattel dolls. Now I happen to have two daughters who are 9 years old and I know what little kids do with dolls. They kiss little dolls and when the Chinese bought Mattel or bought the rights or Mattel decided to contract with the Chinese, the Chinese came to this company and he described how he had to make sure he had the right kind of paint that would not be at all risky to the health of the consumer. And sure enough, they decided to go forward with their own formula and Mattel dolls after about a year were found to have lead paint. And so you have all these little children kissing their doll, thinking and with Americans having trusted Mattel, a very trusted label and not to do something like that, but those children were being put at risk because Mattel had decided to manufacture in China.

By the way, that situation was cleared up, only because it took a huge fight and it took a great amount of spotlighting the issue for that to happen. I think this has been a very good hearing. Do either of you have another question you would like to throw up? I think we could have a second round.

Mr. STOCKMAN. Mr. Chairman, I just want to say something quick. I think we on this panel probably have both conservatives and liberals and are in general agreement. And I think that is an unusual circumstance where we have this concern from both sides of the aisle and both different philosophies. I just again can't stress enough, I think somehow your organizations need to announce that this hearing occurred, and the things that you said and with us also stating that maybe we will generate some interest. This is a very serious issue. And it is alarming that everything that we read now on the labels, in fact, may not be true. And that is what we rely on, those labels. So again, thank you for the hearing, Mr. Chairman

Mr. ROHRABACHER. I will end it with this, obviously from what we have heard today, the American people are facing a threat, a major threat to their well being. Their health, the health of their families could be in great jeopardy and this could be—and they could be put in jeopardy. They may be put in jeopardy by number one, unscrupulous people who are making money dealing with people in China who are not doing anything up to the standard that we expect here in the United States of America.

Mr. KASTEL. And if I can interrupt to add one more thing, Mr. Chairman? Taking off from what you are saying because you are spot on.

Mr. ROHRABACHER. Go right ahead.

Mr. KASTEL. I think we need to hold the businesses in this country that are doing the importing responsible as well because they are again part of this dynamic that places really responsible food producers in the United States at a competitive disadvantage. I use one example, Eden Foods in Clinton, Michigan.

Mr. ROHRABACHER. Say that again?

Mr. KASTEL. Eden Foods in Clinton, Michigan, you asked about Walmart organics, the canned beans at Walmart whether they are pinto beans or black beans, they come from China. Eden Foods buys not from some broker with a piece of paper, but from farmers that they have dealt with for generations in North America, mostly in Michigan, but some in the Plains States and Canada. They know the farmers. They are a little bit more expensive, but they are operating in a very high, ethical level. We need to protect those kind of investors and entrepreneurs and that means that we need to hold responsible for everybody in the supply chain.

If somebody comes in from China at 30 percent cheaper, we need to find out why and those businesses need to do their due diligence. And if they can't inspect, if they are not allowed to go to that factory or those farms, they shouldn't be doing business there.

Mr. ROHRABACHER. Well, step one seems to be for us all to agree, Republican and Democrat, that we believe the consumer has a right to know what they are buying and has a right to know what country of origin they are coming from because consumers may or may not want to deal with—even if it was not healthy, maybe they want to deal with slave labor for countries that don't permit unions or don't permit their workers to earn a decent living. And maybe there are people who are nationalistic and just want to buy from the United States of America, from fellow Americans. That's fine, too. Maybe they are willing to buy a little bit more or pay a little bit more.

So we can all agree that we, as Americans, have a right to make the decisions in our lives based on a free flow of information and accurate information and that right now that is not happening. And in fact, the fact that we have got threatening foods coming in that could do harm to our families suggest to us that the American people are being betrayed by a compromise of standards and someone is making a lot of money at it. I certainly believe that we should be holding the corporate interests, the individuals and the corporations that are pushing for this and bringing food over that may or may not be safe.

And by the way, they are the same ones, when we start talking about labeling, you can bet that these are the folks who have been fighting it behind the scenes the whole time. It is like and I always complain about the companies that go over to China and then the corporate leaders say well, it is not our job to watch out for the security of the United States. That is your job. You pass the laws and we will have to obey them. Until then, we want to invest wherever we want for the benefit of our company, except they don't add that their company then spends a lot of money on lobbying to make sure that we don't pass any laws that prevent them from doing business with a dictatorship that is the world's worst human rights abuser in the world.

So we have got our work cut out for us. This is a very good start in the discussion and I do plan to hold another hearing on this some time in the near future.

Mr. STOCKMAN. Mr. Chairman. I have a request, if possible, could we bring the officials from the Silk Company before the committee?

Mr. ROHRABACHER. We can ask anybody to come here that we would like.

Mr. STOCKMAN. I would like to put Mark and them on the same panel.

Mr. TRIPLETT. Mr. Chairman, one last thing to pick up on the distinguished gentleman's point. We have the names of products and we know people are making a lot of profits. That is exactly what you said. But we don't have the names of who those people are. If, God forbid, we should have a disaster here, stopping all trade is all we have. We don't know who the corrupt officials are. We don't know yet who the people are who are engaged in this. And to the extent that we can gain some information from the administration, task the administration to find the names, that is useful.

I think the Congress did a very good job of naming some Russian officials, you remember, very recently. This is legislation you all did. And it caused a big impact in Russia. You can cause a really big impact in China if you named names or threatened to do so. And that would mean oh gee, I can't go to the United States. I can't visit my money and I can't send my kid to college, all of this kind of thing in the United States. If you begin with the basic data of who the perpetrators are, I think that would be a very useful thing for the committee to do, based on the Russian experience. Thank you.

Mr. ROHRABACHER. Well, transparency and accountability are two essential ingredients if we are going to have freedom and be able to have decent lives and have any security in our lives at all with freedom. Freedom means that you are going to have some choices. Freedom means there is going to be people doing things that you are not totally in control of, but you should be in control of your own decisions. So with that said, I want to thank the panelists for opening up this area of discussion. As I say, I think we will probably have another round of hearings on this some time in the months ahead, but I think we have started the national dialogue which is important. This hearing is adjourned.

[Whereupon, at 3:17 p.m., the subcommittee was adjourned.]

APPENDIX

SUBCOMMITTEE HEARING NOTICE
COMMITTEE ON FOREIGN AFFAIRS
U.S. HOUSE OF REPRESENTATIVES
WASHINGTON, DC 20515-6128

Subcommittee on Europe, Eurasia, and Emerging Threats
Dana Rohrabacher (R-CA), Chairman

May 8, 2013

TO: MEMBERS OF THE COMMITTEE ON FOREIGN AFFAIRS

You are respectfully requested to attend an OPEN hearing of the Subcommittee on Europe, Eurasia, and Emerging Threats in Room 2172 of the Rayburn House Office Building (and available on the Committee website at www.foreignaffairs.house.gov):

DATE: Wednesday, May 8, 2013

TIME: 2:00 p.m.

SUBJECT: The Threat of China's Unsafe Consumables

WITNESSES: Mr. William Triplett II
Author and Consultant
(Former Chief Republican Counsel, Senate Committee on Foreign Relations)

Ms. Patty Lovera
Assistant Director
Food & Water Watch

Mr. Mark Kastel
Co-Founder
The Cornucopia Institute

Ms. Sophie Richardson
China Director
Human Rights Watch

By Direction of the Chairman

The Committee on Foreign Affairs seeks to make its facilities accessible to persons with disabilities. If you are in need of special accommodations, please call 202/225-5021 at least four business days in advance of the event, whenever practicable. Questions with regard to special accommodations in general (including availability of Committee materials in alternative formats and assistive listening devices) may be directed to the Committee.

COMMITTEE ON FOREIGN AFFAIRS

MINUTES OF SUBCOMMITTEE ON _____ *Europe, Eurasia, and Emerging Threats* _____ HEARING

Day_ *Wednesday* _Date_____ *May 8, 2013* _____Room_ *2172 Rayburn HOB*

Starting Time ____ *2:08 pm* ____Ending Time __ *3:17 pm*

Recesses | *n/a* | (____to____)(____to____)(____to____)(____to____)(____to____)(____to____)

Presiding Member(s)

Chairman Dana Rohrabacher

Check all of the following that apply:

Open Session ☑   Electronically Recorded (taped) ☑
Executive (closed) Session ☐   Stenographic Record ☑
Televised ☑

TITLE OF HEARING:

The Threat of China's Unsafe Consumables

SUBCOMMITTEE MEMBERS PRESENT:

Chairman Dana Rohrabacher, Ranking Member William Keating, and Rep. Steve Stockman.

NON-SUBCOMMITTEE MEMBERS PRESENT: *(Mark with an * if they are not members of full committee.)*

None

HEARING WITNESSES: Same as meeting notice attached? Yes ☑ No ☐
(If "no", please list below and include title, agency, department, or organization.)

STATEMENTS FOR THE RECORD: *(List any statements submitted for the record.)*

Prepared Statement of Mr. William Triplett II
Prepared Statement of Ms. Patty Lovera
Prepared Statement of Mr. Mark Kastel
Human Rights Watch Report, "My Children Have Ben Poisoned." Submitted by Sophie Richardson
Human Rights Watch Report, "Promises Unfulfilled: An Assessment of China's National Human Rights Action Plan." Submitted by Sophie Richardson
"China's Public Health Whitewash," June 23, 2010, The Guardian. Submitted by Sophie Richardson

TIME SCHEDULED TO RECONVENE _____
or
TIME ADJOURNED ____ *3:17 pm* ____

Subcommittee Staff Director

F

MATERIAL SUBMITTED FOR THE RECORD BY MS. SOPHIE RICHARDSON, CHINA
DIRECTOR, HUMAN RIGHTS WATCH

[NOTE: The above report is not reprinted here in its entirety but is available in committee records or may be accessed on the Internet at: http://www.hrw.org/sites/default/files/reports/china0611WebInsidel0l0.pdf (accessed 6/5/13).]

CHINA

Promises Unfulfilled

An Assessment of China's National Human Rights Action Plan

HUMAN
RIGHTS
WATCH

[NOTE: The above report is not reprinted here in its entirety but is available in committee records or may be accessed on the Internet at: http://www.hrw.org/sites/default/files/reports/china0111webwcover.pdf (accessed 6/5/13).]

the guardian

Search

China's public health whitewash

International organisations are complicit in China's efforts to hush up the milk contamination scandal during the Olympics

Phelim Kine
theguardian.com, Wednesday 23 June 2010 10.00 BST

Milk labelled to show it has been tested to be free of melamine in China. Photograph: STR/AFP/GettyImages

Pretend it didn't happen. That's apparently the strategy of the Chinese government, the World Health Organisation, and the International Olympic Committee toward China's melamine milk contamination scandal during the Beijing Olympics.

An official ban on reporting of "all food safety issues" during the games stifled domestic media coverage of revelations that at least 20 dairy firms were spiking milk products with the chemical melamine. That cover-up contributed to the deaths of six children and illness among 300,000 others.

But there's not a whisper of melamine – or of the reporting ban – in a May 2010 book jointly issued by the Chinese government, the WHO and IOC, The Health Legacy of the 2008 Beijing Olympic Games: Successes and Recommendations.

That publication instead declares that "no major outbreak of food-borne disease occurred during the Beijing Olympics". The book describes, without irony, the Chinese government's attention to food safety during the Beijing Olympics as "an instructive example of how mass events can be organised to promote health in a value-added way".

The book's introduction features tributes from the IOC president, Jacques Rogge, who praises the Beijing Olympics for providing a "lasting legacy to the benefit of the population in and around Beijing". The WHO director-general, Margaret Chan, commends the Beijing Games for spurring "innovative measures to protect the health of visitors and the local population".

The WHO's and IOC's parroting of the Chinese government's rosy assessment of the Beijing Olympics' health legacy doesn't just defy the historical record. It adds insult to the injury of China's child melamine victims by whitewashing the role of official censorship in their misery. China's state-controlled media was not allowed to publish the melamine contamination story until September 2008. This fact goes unmentioned in the book.

Nor is there a discussion of ongoing persecution of some public health advocates. On 30 March 2010, Zhao Lianhai was hauled before a Beijing court in a one-day closed trial on charges of "provoking disorder" for blowing the whistle on the government's failure to assist the thousands who became ill. Zhao helped to establish a grassroots advocacy group, Home for Kidney Stones Babies, which rallied parents of sick children to demand official compensation and an official day of remembrance. For his efforts, Zhao faces a possible prison term of up to five years.

The Chinese government has a long history of denying or covering up issues it broadly defines as "sensitive" – even public health emergencies. The government stifled public disclosure of its severe acute respiratory syndrome (Sars) outbreak to ensure a crisis-free meeting of the National People's Congress in early 2003.

That decision helped fuel an epidemic, which spread to 25 other countries and killed 774 people before it was contained in July 2003. Two years later, the government blocked all domestic media reports of the massive spill of the toxic chemical benzene in the Songhua river in Heilongjiang province until wild rumours about the disaster prompted disclosure of what had actually happened.

If the WHO is genuinely committed to "the attainment by all people of the highest possible level of health" – its stated objective – it should examine the good, the bad, and the ugly in China, not put its imprimatur on half-truths and cover-ups as to the real health legacy of the Beijing Olympics. The WHO reflected some discomfort when Human Rights Watch inquired about its co-authorship. An email from the WHO's regional office of the western Pacific defends the book as a "scientific study", but adds that its contents "do not necessarily reflect WHO's views, nor does WHO necessarily endorse them".

The IOC's complicity is no less shameful, but less surprising given its well-documented tolerance of the Chinese government's unrelenting campaign to squelch legal peaceful protests, limit media freedom and restrict the internet access of journalists ahead of and during the Beijing Olympics.

The WHO and the IOC owe China's citizens and the international community the truth and not some selective and rosy portrayal dressed up as "science". The WHO should undertake independent reporting on the Beijing Olympics' public health legacy in its monthly medical bulletin. The IOC should integrate ethical principles based on the values enshrined in the Olympic charter to establish human rights-compatible standards to guide the Olympic movement and the selection of future Olympic host cities. And both should demand that the Chinese government immediately release Zhao, stop harassing those seeking redress and allocate necessary funds for their compensation and medical treatment.

That would be an Olympic legacy worth writing about.